Jossey-Bass Teacher

Jossey-Bass Teacher provides educators with practical knowledge and tools to create a positive and lifelong impact on student learning. We offer classroom-tested and research-based teaching resources for a variety of grade levels and subject areas. Whether you are an aspiring, new, or veteran teacher, we want to help you make every teaching day your best.

From ready-to-use classroom activities to the latest teaching framework, our value-packed books provide insightful, practical, and comprehensive materials on the topics that matter most to K–12 teachers. We hope to become your trusted source for the best ideas from the most experienced and respected experts in the field.

This book is delightfully dedicated to my fabulous family: my loving husband, Robert, and my sensational sons, Hart and Devon.

You instilled in me that can-do spirit. You taught me the value of teamwork in learning and life!

The Co-Teaching Book of Lists

Katherine Perez, Ed.D.

Foreword by Harry K. Wong

JOSSEY-BASS
A Wiley Imprint
www.josseybass.com

Published by Jossey-Bass
A Wiley Imprint
One Montgomery Street, Suite 1200, San Francisco, CA 94104-4594—www.josseybass.com

Jossey-Bass books and products are available through most bookstores. To contact Jossey-Bass directly call our Customer Care Department within the U.S. at 800-956-7739, outside the U.S. at 317-572-3986, or fax 317-572-4002.

Library of Congress Cataloging-in-Publication Data

Perez, Katherine D.
    The co-teaching book of lists / Katherine Perez ; foreword by Harry Wong. — 1st ed.
        p. cm. — (Jossey-Bass teacher)
      Includes bibliographical references and index.
    ISBN 978-1-118-01744-9 (pbk.)
    ISBN 978-1-118-22197-6 (ebk.)
    ISBN 978-1-118-23610-9 (ebk.)
    ISBN 978-1-118-26058-6 (ebk.)
  1. Teaching teams. I. Title.
    LB1029.T4P47 2012
    371.14′8—dc23
                                                                        2012010366

Printed in the United States of America

FIRST EDITION
PB Printing 10 9 8 7 6 5 4 3 2 1

Contents

Chapter 1   Co-Teaching in a Nutshell

Chapter 2   Co-Teaching Models

Chapter 3   Where Do You Start?

Chapter 4   Where Do You Go? A Co-Teaching Road Map

Chapter 5   Collaboration: Working as a Team

Chapter 6   Organizing and Planning for Success

Chapter 7 Schoolwide Organization: Administrative Issues

Chapter 8   Accommodations and Modifications That Make a Difference

Chapter 9   Instructional Strategies for Different Types of Learners

Chapter 10   Reflecting on Practice and Planning Tools

About the Author

Katherine Perez, Ed.D., an award-winning classroom teacher, administrator, educational consultant, and speaker, has worked with students from preschoolers to college graduates. Kathy is currently a professor of education at Saint Mary's College of California, director of teaching leadership, and coordinator of professional development and outreach. She specializes in instructional strategies and creative approaches to literacy, learning, and leadership development.

In her books and her teacher workshops, Kathy integrates state-of-the art methods and research with passion and practical insights from her extensive experience as a general educator, special educator, literacy coach, and curriculum and staff development coordinator. She has worked extensively with teachers, administrators, and parents throughout the United States, Canada, Europe, Caribbean, New Zealand and Australia, Hong Kong, and Singapore. Kathy's previous books include *100+ Brain Friendly Tools and Strategies for Literacy* (Corwin, 2010). To learn more, go to www.katherineperez.com.

Acknowledgments

I want to acknowledge those who have helped me along the way in the production of this book.

Thank you to my family for your faithful support—giving me a quiet space to write, being patient with my early mornings and late nights, cooking meals for me while I was writing, and helping me feed the ducks and taking long walks along the lagoon when I needed a break.

While my family fueled me with support and inspiration, my editor, Margie McAneny, propelled me through the publishing process. Through her wisdom, she saw the need for this book and shared her talents, time, and energy to make it a reality. In addition, thanks to Tracy Gallagher, senior editorial assistant, who advised me on clarifying content and provided practical publishing pointers. Both of them helped me navigate the journey of this book, steering me from tips to techniques that transform teaching.

A special thanks to my dear friend and professional colleague, Dr. Harry Wong. Harry is truly a teacher's teacher and mentor to us all!

Finally, I want to thank all of the hundreds of students and teachers I have worked with in my thirty-plus years as a professional educator. You were the fuel that ignited my passion for teaching!

Foreword

By Harry K. Wong

Congratulations on selecting a book that will change your life and the lives of your students. Imagine the Energizer Bunny with a shot of 5-Hour Energy and you have Dr. Kathy Perez. I'm shy, so I sit on the side with her husband, Robert, who is also shy, and we watch as Kathy regales the workshop participants with her panache, style, and charm. Everyone is smiling and engaged when Kathy works her audience. Kathy's passion for teaching and her dedication to the profession are infectious. She did the same when she paired with my wife, Rosemary, as study buddies as they earned their doctorate degrees together.

This book, *The Co-Teaching Book of Lists*, will regale you, as Kathy has poured her academic elegance and expertise into a book that will make you feel like you have a study buddy teaching you how to co-teach a class.

Kathy Perez has dedicated her teaching career to helping *all* students succeed. I have known Kathy for over thirty years, an incredible professional journey that we have shared through the years. Kathy and I have done workshops, separately, in Singapore, a nation that rates among the top-performing countries in the work in student achievement. On other occasions, I have also been in Singapore to oversee the printing of Rosemary's and my book, *The First Days of School*, where, as of this writing, over three million copies have been printed. No matter whether we are in schools, in a printing plant, or shopping in a store, there is a word all Singaporeans use naturally. The word is *colleague*. They never say *I*. As a result, co-teaching, collaboration, and professional learning teams are natural phenomena in Singapore.

The other country that has been dominating the headlines with high student achievement is Finland. Their sustained excellence can be attributed to one word: *trust*. There is a high level of trust for the professionalism of teachers to determine the curriculum, teach the kids, and solve their own problems.

The American educational system is obsessed with a never-ending evaluation testing mode, not trusting teachers. Finland has a mandatory nationwide testing program: it consists of one test given at the end of a senior's high school career. Finland's educational policies are largely in the hands of those they trust—the educators—and the country is now a world leader.

Kathy is an award-winning classroom teacher, administrator, and author. She has worked successfully with students from preschoolers to graduate students and is currently a professor of education—a teacher's teacher—at Saint Mary's College of California, where she is the director of teaching leadership and the coordinator of professional development and outreach.

Her multifaceted journey in education has prepared her well to write this comprehensive book on co-teaching. Because of her vast and diverse experiences, even the most reluctant learners are engaged with her techniques.

In this book, *The Co-Teaching Book of Lists*, both special educators and general educators will find a comprehensive collection of effective resources and techniques that will make a definite difference in their classrooms.

Historically, teaching has been an isolated profession. The teacher goes into the classroom, closes the door, and hopes for the best. Without a culture of collegial support and trust from politicians, policy makers and many administrators, the challenges of meeting the unique needs of diverse learners can be a daunting one. In the past, a specialist would "pull out" students with special needs for remedial work in another room. This further isolated the student and stigmatized him or her in front of the student's peer group. Curriculum coherence suffered as well, unless the teachers involved clearly communicated their goals in a school that values and has a culture of collegiality and collaboration.

With inclusion of special needs students in the classroom, general education teachers were trying their best, but not always succeeding to educate mixed-ability students in their classrooms. They lacked consistent support and the knowledge of adaptations and modifications to the curriculum that would maximize the potential of all of their students.

Teachers, parents, and administrators were not satisfied with this fragmented approach to meeting individual needs in isolation. Kathy Perez knew that something needed to be done. The effectiveness of school-based collaborative activities, with co-teaching being one example, began to be documented in the research literature and in practice. Co-teaching led to results that were valued by students, their teachers, parents, administrators, and the community. Positive outcomes included improved academic and social skills of lower-performing students and greater job satisfaction of the teachers involved. Other results included improved attitudes in students with disabilities and more positive peer relationships. Co-teachers reported professional growth, personal support, and an enhanced collaborative community at the school.

However, one drawback was the lack of professional development, resources, and training available on successful practices and models. This is precisely the special contribution that *The Co-Teaching Book of Lists* brings to the profession.

The ideas in this book are easily accessed and ready to use from planning to implementation. What a terrific tool kit this book represents. *The Co-Teaching Book of Lists* belongs on *every* teacher's bookshelf. You will likely be as impressed as I was with the range of instructional strategies and creative, collaborative approaches to teaching and learning contained in this handy resource. Teachers from all grade levels and subject areas will benefit from the innovative and informative approaches in this book, which can be used immediately.

Both general education and special education teachers will now have at their fingertips a plethora of possibilities to make co-teaching more successful. This valuable book puts together a comprehensive collection of models, strategies, techniques, modifications, and adaptations to choose from in order to customize a successful and collaborative co-teaching program.

May you and your colleagues enjoy co-teaching in an atmosphere of trust.

Harry K. Wong, Ed.D.
Author, *The First Days of School*

Preface

In 1940, the superintendent of the Cincinnati public schools, George Reavis, wrote a fable. Titled *The Animal School*, it's now in the public domain. The fable is very insightful with respect to children who learn differently. As the story illustrates, in many cases it is not the child who is "disabled," but the *educational* system.

Although I have adapted the fable somewhat, the message remains as true today as it was decades ago. I'm going to share the fable with you, and as you read it, see what insights you can gain. Does this fable have a moral for co-teaching?

The Animal School: A Fable

Once upon a time the animals had a school. They had four subjects—running, climbing, flying, and swimming—and all animals took all subjects.

The duck was good at swimming—better than the teacher, in fact. He made passing grades in running and flying, and he was almost hopeless in climbing. So they made him drop swimming to practice more climbing. But average is still OK, and nobody worried about it much—except the duck.

The eagle was considered a troublemaker. In his climbing class, he beat everybody to the top of the tree, but he had his own way of getting there, which was against the rules. He always had to stay after school and write, "Cheating is wrong" three hundred times. This kept him from soaring, which he dearly loved. But schoolwork comes first.

The bear flunked out because they said he was lazy, especially in the winter. His best time was summer, but school wasn't open then.

The penguin never went to school because he couldn't leave home, and they wouldn't start a school out where he lived.

The zebra played hooky a lot. The ponies made fun of his stripes, and this made him very sad.

The kangaroo started out at the top of the running class, but got discouraged trying to run on all fours like the other kids.

The fish quit school because he was bored. To him, all four subjects were the same, but nobody understood that. They had never been a fish.

The squirrel got As in climbing, but his flying teacher made him start from the ground up, instead of the treetop down. His legs got so sore practicing takeoffs that he began getting Cs in climbing and Ds in running.

But the bee was the biggest problem of all, so the teacher sent him to Dr. Owl for testing. Dr. Owl said that the bee's wings were just too small for flying, and, besides, they were in the wrong place. However, the bee never saw Dr. Owl's report, so he just went ahead and flew anyway.

I think I know a bee or two—how about you?

Source: G. Reavis, *The Animal School* (Peterborough, NH: Crystal Springs, 1999).

Remember—fairness does not mean everybody gets the same thing; fairness means everybody gets what they need to be successful!

The Co-Teaching
Book of Lists

Introduction

As special education has evolved over the past twenty-five years, more and more students are taught in the "least restrictive environment" of the general education classroom. Co-teaching is one key service delivery option for special needs students.

This book is written for both teachers and administrators. The strategies presented will encourage and support educators who want to develop a collaborative co-teaching model to serve students with diverse learning needs.

Current research and practice indicate that although students with disabilities may learn best in inclusive classrooms,[1] many general education teachers are unfamiliar with specific strategies of intervention for these students and collaborative strategies in working with special education teachers.

My goal in writing *The Co-Teaching Book of Lists* is to provide practical techniques that will make the co-teaching process more successful for both the teachers involved—as well as for the students. We know that students learn best in classrooms that include a variety of lesson formats reflecting individual learning styles.[2] Drawing upon my thirty-five years as a professional educator in both special education and general education classrooms, this book offers a much-needed instructional tool kit for collaborative teaching and student success.

The book presents positive and practical ideas for working together in today's inclusive classrooms. The format is easily accessible, with checklists and other activities and resources to help teachers design a successful collaborative program.

In today's diverse schools, change is needed. Traditionally, teaching has been an isolating profession, with one teacher in a separate classroom instructing his or her own students. Many experts have noted that traditional "pull-out" programs do not adequately prepare students with disabilities for their real-life experiences after school. The trend is to implement modifications in the general class setting, which requires teachers to be more flexible, creative, and collaborative. Teachers will therefore benefit from this book's advice on scaffolding, adaptations, accommodations, and interventions for a co-teaching situation.

The Knowledge Base Behind This Book

This book is meant to be a practical guide for a successful co-teaching program, not a theoretical textbook, but all the strategies and ideas presented here are research-based and teacher-tested. Many of the ideas are based on the work of Tomlinson, Marzano, Friend, Winebrenner, Gardner, Armstrong, and Jensen.

How the Book Is Organized

The Co-Teaching Book of Lists is organized into ten chapters. Each of the chapters can be read and referenced independently. All the chapters are loaded with ideas, tips, and tools to assist you in your journey of co-teaching.

Let the journey begin!

Chapter 1

Co-Teaching in a Nutshell

List 1.1   Characteristics of Co-Teaching

Co-teaching involves two professionals (usually a special education teacher and a general educator) working together to share in the planning, instructing, and ongoing assessment of a group of students. This model has also been adopted in delivering instruction to other diverse populations including at-risk learners, advanced learners, and English learners. The key components of co-teaching are:

- Two or more professionals working together in one classroom
- Both (or all) teachers actively involved with students in whole-group and small-group instruction
- Delivering instruction collaboratively to students with diverse needs
- Two teachers physically present in heterogeneous classrooms, with joint and equal responsibility for instruction
- Both teachers sharing the leadership role in the classroom
- Communication and collaboration becoming priorities
- Both (or all) teachers sharing in planning and assessing processes
- Continuum of services depending on the needs of the students
- Instruction delivered primarily in a single classroom setting
- Teachers sharing joint ownership of class, resources, and accountability

However, having two teachers in the same classroom is not all that co-teaching means; it requires co-planning, co-instruction, and co-assessment.

List 1.2   What Co-Teaching Is

- In the general education classroom
- More than one professional to support students
- Cooperative learning and collaboration for the teachers
- An opportunity for endless possibilities
- Dependent upon co-planning and co-scheduling

Therefore, *co-teaching* is two or more professionals working together to provide instruction to students in an inclusive setting.

- Teachers plan together, instruct the class together, and collaborate for assessment, grading, and differentiating instruction
- In an ideal setting, teachers have common planning time to facilitate their work together for inclusion
- Co-teaching allows teachers to meet the needs of struggling and advanced learners in the classroom
- Students learn from two or more people who may have different ways of thinking and teaching
- Co-teaching is a creative and collaborative way to connect with and support others in helping all students succeed in the classroom
- Co-teaching helps make schools more effective

Co-Teaching in a Nutshell

List 1.3   What Co-Teaching Is Not

We just discussed the key elements of the co-teaching process. The elements listed in the preceding list need to be in place for a successful co-teaching program. However, because of the many misconceptions about the co-teaching process, we should also explore what co-teaching is not:

- Co-teaching is not easy
- Co-teaching is not the only way
- Co-teaching is not right for everyone in every situation
- Co-teaching is not a remedial classroom
- Co-teaching is not a way to "fix" weak teachers
- Co-teaching is not playing "tag team" in the classroom, with one teacher teaching one subject and the other teacher teaching the next subject without mutual coordination
- Co-teaching is not one teacher at the copy machine, correcting papers, or doing secretarial support while the other teacher provides direct instruction in the classroom
- Co-teaching is not one teacher delivering a lesson while the other decorates a desk or holds up a wall on the sidelines and watches; co-teaching requires that both certified teachers are directly involved in providing instruction and supporting student learning in the classroom
- Co-teaching is not two teachers deciding to combine their classes together to teach a lesson or a unit; this approach is called team teaching and may be valuable for certain projects, but it is not co-teaching
- Co-teaching is not occurring when one teacher dominates the discussion or instruction as the leading authority or prevails in decisions about what is to be taught
- Co-teaching is not inclusion, and inclusion is not co-teaching. These two terms are often used interchangeably. Inclusion is a philosophical practice in which a multitude of diverse learners of mixed ability are taught in the same classroom. Co-teaching is just one way to implement inclusion.
- Co-teaching is not designating one of the partners as a tutor to assist and support the general education teacher only with struggling students.
- Co-teaching is not happening when the special education teacher is in and out of the classroom inconsistently and therefore does not have a way to deliver instruction on a regular basis. In this situation, the general education teacher does not have an opportunity to share responsibilities for planning and delivering instruction and cannot count on the special education teacher as a partner. The special education teacher becomes more of a consultant instead of a co-teacher.

List 1.4   Framework for Co-Teaching

Many elements influence a co-teaching program's ability to successfully teach *diverse learners.*

School Culture

- Collaborative, collegial ways of working together
- Collective vision of an inclusive school
- Commitment to shared vision and beliefs
- System of traditions and rituals

Organization

- Dedicated and informed leadership
- Collaborative scheduling
- Ongoing professional development
- Adequate facilities
- Sufficient resources

Collaboration

- Time for reflection
- Tapping into strengths and talents of each teacher
- Clearly defined roles and responsibilities
- Attributes and beliefs of individual teachers
- Utilizing all available resources

Instruction

- Scheduling and planning
- Adaptations and modifications
- Ongoing assessment and grading
- Differentiated instruction
- Use of multiple intelligences
- Whole- and small-group activities
- Realistic expectations
- Adequate use of space
- Carefully defined procedures and routines
- Selection of appropriate co-teaching models

List 1.5   How Co-Teaching Benefits Teachers

When done properly, co-teaching can be one of the most innovative practices in education. The exchange of knowledge and skills among team members and higher teacher-student ratios are some of the main benefits of implementing this process.

In a co-teaching classroom that fully utilizes the expertise of both teachers, students are more likely to achieve more and remain on task more than they would be in a traditional pullout segregated program. Some of the other benefits include:

- Students with learning and behavior problems are surrounded by positive peer models in the general education classroom, and their behavior will most likely improve. This greatly facilitates classroom management for teachers.
- Educators who have experienced co-teaching find that they are more energized and creative, are able to trust one another, and have more fun teaching.[1]
- Co-teaching encourages teachers to share expertise, providing one another with valuable feedback.[2]
- Teachers involved in co-teaching relationships state that this relationship results in increased professional satisfaction, opportunities for professional growth, personal support, and opportunities for collaboration.[3]
- Co-teaching enhances any needed whole-group instruction while still meeting individual needs.[4]
- The value added by having a special education teacher in the room to co-teach results in more individual attention for students, more on-task student behavior, and more interaction with teachers.[5]
- Special education teachers gain insight into the realities of the general classroom while general educators learn valuable lessons in planning, accommodating, and instructing students with learning or behavioral difficulties.[6]
- Co-teaching makes it easier to conduct hands-on activities and provide flexible testing situations.[7]

List 1.6 Advantages for the General Education Teacher

- Learning opportunities to reach *all* students
- Background information gained on special education
- More time to focus on content and less on individual problems
- Increased awareness of the extent of students' academic difficulties and ways to support diverse student learning
- Specific skills of the special education teacher's to match students' individual learning styles
- Awareness of different successful learning strategies
- More time to learn, share, and use learning strategies
- More focused techniques to help special education students
- Background information on special education students provided
- Assistance with nonidentified students who also need strategic support—assistance for *all* students, labels or not
- Support for students who need organizational strategies
- Feedback available from special educator on content presentation
- Student peer pressure in favor of appropriate behavior, so that inappropriate behavior is decreased
- Work together with special educator for home-school support
- Twice as much opportunity for teacher's assistance
- Professional growth opportunity and greater personal satisfaction
- Students organizational skills and efforts monitored by special education teacher
- More time for personal necessity breaks—like going to the bathroom!

List 1.7　Advantages for the Special Education Teacher

- Special education teacher's increased understanding of goings-on in the general education classroom
- More time-effective
- Specific content area specialization not needed
- Ability to learn the expectations of the general education classroom by teaching alongside a subject-matter expert
- More opportunities to use specialized intervention skills with more students
- More time to help students develop motivation, social skills, effort, and responsibility for their own learning
- Greater awareness of student progress and student performance throughout the day, so teachers are more in touch with students
- Knowing the daily procedures and routines of the general education teacher
- Having more time to use learning strategies within subject areas and to help students transfer and generalize information
- More realistic goals can be set for special needs students with increased exposure to "normalcy"
- Improved student behaviors
- "Reality check" for student goals within the general education setting
- More positive feedback from parents
- Rewards of seeing students succeed and establish credibility among peers
- More positive teacher-student relationships
- Partnering with a colleague to support IEP goals
- Mutual learning and appreciation for each other's expertise
- Professional growth and greater personal satisfaction

List 1.8　Advantages of Co-Teaching for Students

When students are provided with proper supports and learning strategies, they receive the benefits of a content expert providing instruction combined with the benefits of a learning strategies expert offering necessary interventions, scaffolding, and modifications for success.

- Positive social outcomes for students with and without disabilities[8]
- Behavioral and academic expectations still high for students[9]
- More individual attention and more interaction with teachers for all students[10]
- Increased student engagement and increased use of strategies by students[11]
- Increased self-confidence and self-esteem, enhanced academic performance, increased social skills and stronger peer relations for all students[12]
- Exposure to the different teaching styles of two teachers
- More difficult for students to go "off task"
- Shorter wait times to get needed help from teachers
- Less fragmented learning that makes more sense

List 1.9   Advantages for the General Education Student

- Strong emphasis on learning skills, organization, and preparedness
- Opportunities for leadership through peer tutoring
- More productive and personalized learning experiences
- More contact time with teachers for greater individualized instruction
- Greater engagement in the classroom
- Enhanced sense of responsibility
- More time spent working cooperatively, acquiring new knowledge, and learning more about ways to make positive contributions in class
- More attention to the development of social skills
- Diverse learning techniques available and more attention to individual learning styles for instruction
- Improved self-esteem
- Better understanding and sensitivity toward students with different abilities
- Unique learning needs met for students with and without disabilities

List 1.10   Advantages for the Special Education Student

- Content expertise and learning strategies expertise offered in tandem, with specific interventions to help students succeed
- Access to the general education curriculum for students with disabilities[13]
- Effort is recognized and valued, so students tend to like school more
- Improved self-esteem
- More meaningful grading and assessment procedures
- More positive attitudes, greater availability of role models for behavior and learning, more interaction with nondisabled peers, and exposure to higher-level concepts and discussions than in segregated special education settings[14]
- Opportunity to learn and grow in the least restrictive environment
- Opportunity to make contributions to the general education classroom
- Strong emphasis on learning skills, organization, and preparedness
- Practice in setting realistic goals
- Enhanced citizenship and sense of responsibility
- More opportunities for reinforcement of classwork when it is presented
- More contact time with teachers for individualized instruction based on student needs
- Less fear of failure and learned helplessness due to experiences with success
- More exposure to students with appropriate behaviors and successful learning skills
- Less stigma for seeking help when services and support are provided inside the classroom

List 1.11   Considerations for Starting a New Co-Teaching Initiative

- Start small and work with teachers who are willing to participate
- Work out issues and schedules carefully in a small group first before going full scale schoolwide; don't start without proper preparation and training or with reluctant teachers
- Provide in-depth professional development that is sustained over time for teachers
- If possible, match up personalities of prospective co-teachers carefully in order to properly implement IEP requirements
- If your school is struggling to find appropriate matches for co-teaching, teachers may need to be flexible by moving to a different grade level or a less preferred schedule

List 1.12   Where Does Co-Teaching Take Place?

Any benefit from co-teaching is diminished when students with special needs are pulled out for instruction in a segregated setting. This may seem like a sensible approach to handling wide gaps in ability levels, but this is *not* co-teaching.

- Students in a separate classroom miss out on class discussions, positive peer role models, and interactions between their teachers; instruction necessary for summative assessment might also be missed during this time.
- Co-teaching usually takes place in *one* classroom.
- Diverse learning needs can be accommodated through the use of flexible grouping, centers, tiered lessons, differentiated instruction, and mixed-ability groups.
- In some cases of alternate teaching, students may be removed to another space for a brief period and then the groups switched, for example, when part of the class is working on very active projects and other students need a quiet space to read and prepare for a test. This is a temporary situation that arises from the needs of the students and the lesson plan.
- It is critical that students remain in the "least restrictive environment," and there needs to be a compelling reason to pull them out of the general education classroom.

The Co-Teaching Book of Lists

List 1.13   Terms Co-Teachers Need to Know

It is important to remember that special education is not a *place,* but rather a set of services.

Accommodations: Changes that allow a person with a disability to participate fully in an activity. Examples include extended time, different test format, and alterations to a classroom.

Adaptations: When instructional materials present a barrier to student learning, teachers often adapt the materials to allow students greater access to the information to be taught. These adaptations may involve changing the content or the format of the materials.

Adequate Yearly Progress (AYP): This represents a state's measure of progress toward meeting state academic standards. "AYP is the minimum level of improvement that states, school districts, and schools must achieve each year."[15]

Asperger Syndrome: A developmental disorder characterized by deficits in social interaction and restricted and unusual patterns of behavior and interests.

Attention Deficit Hyperactivity Disorder or Attention Deficit Disorder (ADHD/ ADD): Neurobiological disorder characterized by distractibility, hyperactivity or impulsive behaviors, and a general inability to focus attention.

Autism: A lifelong developmental disability that usually begins sometime during the first three years of life. It is a neurological disorder that affects communication, social interactions, and perceptions of and reactions to the world.

Central Auditory Processing Disorder (CAPD): A disorder that affects a student's ability to process auditory information.

Cognitively Impaired or Mentally Impaired (CI or MI): Significantly subaverage general intellectual functioning that exists concurrently with deficits in adaptive behavior that adversely affect a student's educational performance.

Continuum of Services: The Individuals with Disabilities Education Act (IDEA) requires each school district to ensure that there is a "continuum of alternative placements" available to meet the needs of students with disabilities. Emphasis should be placed on the provision of services and not the specific placements themselves. This continuum must include general education classes, special education classes, special schools, home instruction, and instruction in hospitals or institutions. This continuum of alternative services *must be* designed to ensure that there is an appropriate setting for each student according to the student's specific needs.

Co-Teaching: An arrangement in which two or more certified educators share planning and instructional responsibility for a single group of diverse learners, primarily in one classroom, for teaching specific content objectives. Although the approaches may vary and the teachers' participation may vary, both teachers have mutual ownership and share resources, planning, assessment, and accountability. Co-teaching is not the same as team teaching or inclusion.

Emotional-Behavioral Disorder (EBD): A student who has normal intelligence, but whose emotional or social behavior inhibits him or her from normal learning.

504 Plan: An accommodation plan for students who have difficulties in school, but do not qualify for special education services at this time.

Functional Behavior Assessment (FBA): A problem-solving process for addressing challenging student behavior. It relies on a variety of techniques and strategies to identify the purposes of specific behavior and to help IEP teams select interventions to directly address the challenging behavior.

Inclusion: This term is not used in IDEA, and the Department of Education has not defined it. However, *inclusion* is generally accepted to mean that primary instruction and provision of services for a child with a disability are provided in an age-appropriate general education class in the school the child would have attended if not disabled, with appropriate additional supports for the student and the teacher. The least restrictive environment (LRE) is the legal basis for inclusion programs, as it strengthens and reinforces the objective of educating all students in a general education classroom to the maximum extent possible.[16]

Individualized Education Plan (IEP): The written plan for each student that defines the academic, social, behavioral, or functional needs of that student.

Individuals with Disabilities Education Act (IDEA): The federal law governing the education of children with disabilities. IDEA and its regulations define the least restrictive environment (LRE) and require that all states demonstrate they have policies and procedures in place to guarantee they meet the federal LRE requirements.

Learning Disability (LD): Average to above average learning potential, with difficulty learning in one or more areas (such as reading or math) and a severe discrepancy between a student's ability and achievement.

Dyscalculia: difficulty with math skills

Dysgraphia: difficulty with written expression

Dyslexia: difficulty reading

Dyspraxia: difficulty with fine motor skills

Least Restrictive Environment (LRE): The Individuals with Disabilities Education Act (IDEA) defines LRE this way: "To the maximum extent appropriate, children with disabilities, including children in public or private institutions or other care facilities are (1) educated with children who are not disabled, and (2) special classes, separate schooling, or other removal of children with disabilities from the regular educational environment occurs only when the nature or severity of the disability of a child is such that education in regular classes with the use of supplementary aids and services cannot be achieved satisfactorily."

Response to Intervention (RTI): RTI involves monitoring student progress to make data-based decisions for students to maximize student achievement. Methods may vary according to the levels of interventions provided. Universal interventions deal with core curriculum in the general education classroom. Secondary interventions involve more intense small-group work. Tertiary interventions are even more focused and provided primarily by a intervention specialist or a special educator. (Office of Special Education and Rehabilitative Services, 2007)

Scaffolding: The teacher provides support in the form of modeling, prompts, direct explanations, and targeted questions—a teacher-guided approach at first. As students begin to master objectives, direct supports are reduced and the learning becomes more independent.

Tourette Syndrome: A disorder that typically involves motor tics and one or more vocal tics at the same time, that occur many times a day over an extended period of time.

List 1.14 Opening Assumptions for Co-Teaching

1. The desired outcomes for students should drive how adults are organized.

2. All students need support to learn. Many of the supports needed today differ substantially from the way existing structures were designed to provide support.

3. Students will be better supported if a team of individuals is responsible for meeting those needs.

4. All educators have unique areas of expertise that are needed by students.

5. Adults in a school system need ongoing access to one another to learn, plan, contribute, feel supported, and share responsibility and accountability for meeting the needs of all learners.

List 1.15 A Co-Teaching Anticipation Guide

Mark A (if you agree) or D (if you disagree) with each of the following statements. You will find discussion guidelines to accompany this guide in the Appendix.

_____ 1. There are many different models for implementing co-teaching in the classroom.

_____ 2. Co-teaching can capitalize on the strengths and areas of expertise of each teacher.

_____ 3. Co-teaching has the most favorable outcomes when teachers get to choose their co-teaching partners.

_____ 4. *Inclusion* and *co-teaching* mean the same thing.

_____ 5. Students generally have positive feelings about being in a co-taught classroom.

_____ 6. Given the opportunity, most teachers embrace the idea of co-teaching.

_____ 7. Grouping students by readiness levels in a co-taught classroom produces stigmatization.

_____ 8. Team teaching is like tag-team teaching: first my turn, then your turn, and so forth.

_____ 9. The groups of students with the special education teacher are always the students with an IEP.

_____ 10. In the one teacher–one support model, one instructor teaches and the other does the grading, copying, and paperwork.

_____ 11. In parallel teaching, a special education teacher is given a lesson plan and may make accommodations and modifications as needed.

_____ 12. In planning a co-taught lesson, the subject matter teacher takes the lead, and the special education teacher focuses in on remediation.

List 1.16   The Beginning Stages of Co-Teaching

- Both teachers actively involved with students in whole-group lessons
- Co-teaching partnerships will emerge
- Teachers share leadership role in the classroom
- Teachers make communication a priority
- Moderate amount of planning required
- Teachers share in planning and assessing
- Itinerate schedules fit into this approach

Chapter 2

Co-Teaching Models

There are many different approaches to collaboration and two teachers working together for a more integrated approach in meeting the needs of all students. These should be seen as implementation tools to choose from depending on the situation, the students, and the teachers involved. These approaches are flexible and should be modified frequently to best meet the needs of the classroom and the curriculum. You always have a choice in the form of collaboration when creating a positive learning environment. Use your own experience as a guide in the cooperative process.

What does co-teaching look like? What are some different approaches to use? Marilyn Friend (2008) has identified six approaches to co-teaching that can be used in collaborative settings[1]. This chapter will use the following terminology identified by Friend to describe these models:

- One teach, one observe
- One teach, one assist
- Team teaching
- Station teaching
- Parallel teaching
- Alternative teaching

Furthermore, additional approaches and variations that are designed for both whole-group and small-group settings will be described.

Level 1   Large-Group Instruction

List 2.1   One Teach, One Observe

- Use this model in new co-teaching situations
- Use this model as an intervention when questions arise about a student's performance
- Use this model to check on student progress
- Use this model to compare target students with others in class
- Let one teacher take the lead in the instruction while the other teacher observes the class or specific target students
- Establish a clear purpose for the observation, with outcomes shared, in order for this model to enhance instructional quality
- Co-teachers decide which types of information to gather during instruction and agree on a method for gathering the data
- Co-teachers should review and analyze the observation information together to decide on instructional implications
- Observation should be a systematic part of the lesson, not just an incidental check of student activities
- The two teachers should take turns observing and teaching and sharing this role
- This may be a suitable approach initially, when the two teachers are getting used to each other and the students in the class
- More in-depth observations of students engaged in the lesson can be made and discussed by the teachers as a follow-up based on the data gathered
- After rapport and collaboration have been established between the two co-teachers, they can observe each other delivering lessons as a form of coaching
- Because it is difficult for a single teacher to teach and collect data at the same time, this approach extends the effectiveness of the lesson for more positive results

Teaching Examples

- Use a blank NCR form or sticky notes to record your observations; then you can share your data immediately with your teacher partner
- Things to look for include observing which students initiate conversations in cooperative groups. Which ones are reticent to respond or do not participate?
- Collect data on which students begin (or do not begin) the work promptly
- Make notes on off-task and on-task behavior
- Use a focus student to determine if their inattentive behavior is less, about the same, or greater than that of the other students in class
- Look for students who are confused or have difficulty processing the information or directions given. What scaffolding techniques can you suggest?

List 2.2   One Teach, One Drift

- Use when one teacher has particular expertise in a certain area
- Helpful at the beginning of a co-teaching relationship to get to know each other's teaching style
- Review lesson—does it lend itself to delivery by one teacher?
- If the lesson is process-oriented and requires direct application on the part of the students, use this method for greater monitoring of student progress
- One teacher takes the lead in instruction while the other teacher roams throughout the classroom to sustain student attention and maintain on-task behavior
- The roaming teacher provides unobtrusive assistance to students as needed, takes the pulse of the class, and makes sure students are on target with the lesson
- Keep in mind that some of this drifting, however, might be distracting to some students
- Although this approach has value, it is sometimes overused by teachers who are reluctant to make changes in their program and delivery of instruction
- Each teacher should have the opportunity to alternately lead instruction, then drift, if this approach is used, to create greater parity in the classroom

Teaching Examples

- Special educator teaches students how to organize their notes for a Civil War report while the general educator circulates among students to offer additional assistance
- Find out how well the students understand the steps in the scientific method
- General educator reviews fraction problems on the board while the special educator walks from group to group to check on worksheets
- Find out whether all students understand a lesson on note taking
- Special educator leads the discussion on the science chapter while the general educator roams around the room and observes whether students are paying attention
- General educator teaches the lesson on the novel while the special educator collects data on the observable behaviors of three target students
- "I have never taught algebra, and I don't know this teacher's style of delivery; I need to drift and understand the flow of the class first"

List 2.3 One Teach, One Assist or Support

- Subject expert is often the lead teacher
- Support teacher is often the specialist
- Support teacher's role defined by student IEPs
- The more time spent planning and collaborating, the more benefit for all in the classroom
- One teacher takes the lead for instruction in this model while the other teacher supports and enhances the instruction
- The support teacher can provide assistance to individual students, use position control to manage behavior, consider ways to reinforce the current lesson later, put additional teaching notes on the board, and ask questions for the students that they might not ask on their own
- After students begin working on the assignment, both teachers circulate around the classroom and provide needed support
- The co-teachers work with as many students as needed
- Since one of the teachers is in a relatively passive role in the classroom, this approach should be used sparingly
- This approach can be very useful when a specialist co-teaches with several different teachers in a day and there is limited planning time
- The specialist helps to implement the general education teacher's curriculum

Teaching Examples

- One teacher presents the content and the other teacher provides a learning strategy or use of manipulatives that supports the acquisition and/or storage of information
- General educator leads a discussion during morning message circle time and special educator assists several students to use their augmentative communication devices to participate
- One teacher presents the content and the other teacher interjects questions or strategies that promote student engagement and information processing
- One teacher is demonstrating the content of the lesson and the other teacher is recording key ideas on the board
- The general educator explains the choice of learning centers for the day and the special educator models and demonstrates the content and process of the centers, as well as the outcomes required
- While one teacher is explaining a chapter in the history book, the other teacher is completing a graphic organizer on the board to reinforce key concepts
- The general educator gives directions for a science project while the special educator checks for understanding and informally assesses the group with a "thumbs up" and "thumbs down" technique—do they understand or do they need more help?
- Special educator reviews the agenda for the day while the general educator checks in with the students for homework completion
- One teacher presents the content and the other teacher provides visual supplements such as graphic organizers to clarify the concept

- General education teacher opens with whole-class instruction about the legislative branch of government; special education teacher follows with a lesson concerning the executive branch; instruction shifts back to the general educator, who discusses the legislative branch; special education teacher finishes the lesson with the system of checks and balances in government

One Teacher, One Support Does Not Look Like . . .

- One teaches and the other sits in the classroom not sure what to do, because there has been too little communication or planning, so both teachers feel a lack of ownership and involvement in the teaching process.
- One is actively involved in teaching and the other does "busywork" like grading, copying, and other paperwork.
- One teacher delivers the lesson to the whole group and the other teacher works in the background monitoring, helping, and keeping students on task. However, the second teacher has no authority to contribute to the lesson or make accommodations or modifications to the lesson and students perceive this lack of power very quickly.

List 2.4   Team Teaching

- Instruction and planning are shared
- Activities and dialogue are coordinated
- Trust, commitment, and personality compatibility are all necessary
- Time and support to plan together are needed
- Both teachers usually need to feel competent in the subject area
- Both teachers teach the class at the same time
- Both teachers teach as one unit, simultaneously delivering and sharing the instruction to the students
- This approach is most dependent on meshing the different teachers' styles
- Co-teachers can equally present the content being taught, ask critical-thinking questions, debate with each other, interject to make a point, and take advantage of each other's knowledge of the subject
- Students clearly see no difference in hierarchy or power between the two teachers using this seamless approach to delivery of instruction
- Teachers often find this approach satisfying, stimulating, and engaging
- Students are usually motivated by this type of "double delivery" in the classroom
- Some co-teachers become so attuned with this method that they feel their workload is reduced and their effectiveness is increased

Team Teaching Does Not Look Like . . .

- Tag-team teaching: my turn, your turn; this can be very distracting to the students
- One teacher teaches while the other teacher uses the time as a prep period

Level 2   Small-Group Instruction

List 2.5   Station Teaching

- Involves the use of learning centers
- Flexible groups: pairs, triads, or small groups
- Instruction is individualized
- Effective format for addressing wide range of abilities
- Standards-based topics with activities at different levels based on student assessments
- Each center is focused on one topic, providing activities at all levels to extend and enrich ideas
- One teacher can facilitate the station, one teacher can check student progress, and a paraprofessional can monitor and reteach
- Possible to arrange one enrichment group, one on-track group, and one review group
- Possible to use three mixed-ability groups with differentiation by process: one hands-on activity, one computer-based activity, and one oral or dramatic activity
- Each teacher facilitates one group; a third group can run independently or with a paraprofessional
- Two teachers provide instruction to different groups of students in different parts of the classroom and divide the content to be taught
- Independent or small-group learning stations can be incorporated into the rotation to extend the learning
- Allows students to work at their own readiness levels
- Students can work in small groups to accelerate their progress in meeting curriculum goals
- Students can choose materials from the stations to work on independently, and the co-teachers become facilitators in their learning
- Teachers can set up two stations and each monitor one station
- Teachers can have one group working on advanced material while another group works on targeted interventions and a third group works independently

Teaching Examples

- Each co-teacher is positioned in a different place in the room
- Each teaches a different set of skills to understand the key concepts of a new science unit
- Each teacher facilitates a group of students through a learning center activity utilizing various learning styles and multiple intelligences; students rotate through the centers and receive instruction from both teachers
- General educator preteaches vocabulary and key concepts of a chapter in social studies through a semantic sort lesson with one group; special educator works with

the other group reinforcing the learning strategy of the week and how they can apply it to the text; after twenty minutes, the groups switch

- The general educator, special educator, and paraprofessional each facilitate a lab station during science class; students rotate, and teachers remain in place
- Each teacher facilitates a small-group word sort game on nouns and adjectives; all students participate in each teacher's group game

Station Teaching Does Not Look Like . . .

- Only the advanced learners or the students with special needs are allowed to use the centers
- The general education teacher creates the centers, and the special education teacher is not aware of the content, purpose, or process of the centers
- All the gifted students placed together, all the grade-level students together, and all the special needs students together for segregated teaching

List 2.6   Parallel Teaching

- Class should be divided in two groups
- Both teachers teach the same content to smaller group
- Teachers should plan together for consistency
- Student mix should be divided carefully
- Two teachers provide the same instruction simultaneously
- One teacher conducts the lesson with half the class, and the other teacher takes the other half
- Student learning is facilitated though closer supervision by the teacher and more opportunities to respond
- Students may be grouped heterogeneously or according to readiness levels
- Students work with only one teacher
- Increases the teacher-student ratio and fosters attention to individual needs
- May also be used to vary learning experiences by providing hands-on manipulatives, for example, to one group and having the other group work on a different process or product
- Possible to have all students reading about the same topic, but at different levels of difficulty

Examples of Teaching

- Using the results of a spelling test, each co-teacher reviews targeted concepts using tiered activities to expand word understanding
- Both teachers plan and design a lesson to implement reciprocal teaching concepts following a story that has been read in heterogeneous groups
- Prior to the beginning of a unit on the oceans, each teacher facilitates a small group discussion utilizing the K-W-L technique (What do we **k**now about the topic? What do we **w**ant to know about the topic? And, after revisiting charts after the unit, What did we **l**earn?)
- As students work in cooperative groups to discuss key concepts of a math lesson, both teachers work with each group
- During English class, students can be divided into two heterogeneous groups; both teachers teach a lesson about metacognitive thinking while reading; then the whole class regroups to practice modeling, guided practice, and reinforcement activities
- Special educator works with a small group of students who are rehearsing a reader's theater script about the story they are reading, and general educator works with another group that is designing a story map to depict the main events of the story

Parallel Teaching Does Not Look Like . . .

- The special educator is given a prewritten lesson plan and has no authority to make accommodations and modifications as necessary; no co-planning was done in the process
- The special needs students with an IEP work with the special education teacher, and other students are with the general education teacher most of the time

The Co-Teaching Book of Lists

List 2.7   Alternative Teaching

- Usually has one large group and one smaller group
- Instructors may teach the same or different content
- Each teacher teaches his or her content, then they switch
- Good approach to use as needed
- Having several small groups for different purposes eliminates some of the stigma of the LD child being singled out
- One teacher provides instruction that is needed by a particular group of students or an individual student, while the other teacher works with the remainder of the class
- The instructional sequence for the individual student or small group usually involves preteaching, reteaching, supplemental instruction, or enrichment
- Process is usually short-term, often for a single class period or a portion of a class period
- Students in need of extra help in specific skills should receive the alternative teaching approach, getting the attention that will help them succeed
- Such smaller groups can be used for remediation or to help students who have been absent to catch up on key instruction and assessment
- The composition of the small group should vary; it should not always be the lowest achievers, as this approach the same drawbacks as segregating and tracking within the class
- This approach can take two forms: in one, the co-teachers divide the class so that one teacher has a larger group and the other teacher has a smaller group; the other form has one teacher teaching one topic while another teacher teaches a different topic and then the students switch
- Co-teachers can thus capitalize on their teaching strengths and preferences; for example, one teacher may prefer teaching organizational skills in writing, while the other teacher prefers to discuss getting ideas for writing
- Students benefit from having multiple teaching styles in the classroom

Examples of Teaching

- Special educator works with a small group of students to teach them a step-by-step process of understanding the scientific method using models and manipulatives
- Special educator leads a large-group discussion while the general educator works with a small group of students who are developing individual learning contracts for a unit in social studies
- Special educator teaches conflict resolution and a social skills lesson while the general educator takes photos of the students and asks them to write a poem about themselves
- One teacher presents a lesson on the principles of long division while the other teacher monitors students working on independent math contracts
- General educator facilitates a pair-share activity to summarize a lesson while the special educator works with a small group on the use of adaptive switches for a word bingo game to be played later in the day

- General educator facilitates and monitors independent contract work by students while the special educator works with a group of students interested in test preparation techniques
- Special educator works with a small group of students on telling time while the rest of the class has a read-aloud time with their cross-age reading buddies
- Using a pretest in math, the general educator works with a small group on long division while the special educator works with another group on simple division and the third group works independently at centers
- The special educator works on book reports with a small group of students while the general educator works with the other group on a choice board to provide alternatives to traditional book reports, according to their learning styles and needs

Alternative Teaching Does Not Look Like...

- The groups of students in the classroom remain relatively static, and the students with an IEP are always with the special education teacher
- The special education teacher is given a lesson plan and has no input on the delivery and no authority to modify it for students with special needs

Source: Model names selected from M. Friend, *Co-Teaching: A Handbook for Creating and Sustaining Successful Classroom Partnerships in Inclusive Schools* (Greensboro, NC: MFI, 2008).

Variations of Models

List 2.8   Skill Group Teaching

- The two co-teachers divide students into several groups, according to instructional needs and readiness levels
- After a period of time, students are reassessed and the groups are rotated so that both teachers have knowledge of all students' academic levels
- Another alternative is to have the special educator visit the classroom only two or three times each week to teach a small group of students a specific skill they may not have mastered; this is not a desirable approach, since the services are not as integrated as in the other models

List 2.9   Speak and Add Model

- One teacher takes the lead in delivering the lesson and the other teacher enriches and extends the content with examples, visual aids, clarifications, questions, and additional support
- The second teacher can also informally assess the learners, check for understanding, and help students stay on task
- Students benefit by hearing two different voices and perspectives on the topics
- Learning is enriched by the visual aids that are created to extend and apply the lesson
- In this collaborative model, teachers are comfortable with each other's teaching styles and can reinforce the key points of the lesson
- For whole-class teaching, this model is effective in sharing the content to be delivered
- Students who are confused or need to refocus can benefit from this approach during coaching

Benefits

When using this approach, teachers:

- Provide on-the-spot feedback and clarification of key concepts
- Are able to informally assess and monitor student learning
- Support more active participation

List 2.10   Duet Teaching

- Both teachers co-plan and co-teach the lesson, using varying co-teaching presentation approaches to enhance student engagement and small-group instruction opportunities
- In many ways, this structure is the most comprehensive of all of the approaches
- Both teachers are actively involved in the planning process and decide on the curriculum goals and outcomes of the lesson
- This model lends itself to differentiation as teachers combine their expertise and instructional strategies
- Teachers need to know the students well and be able to modify curriculum on the spot to meet individual needs in this approach
- Students feel included as instruction becomes the focus and the importance of labels diminishes
- This approach takes time to be effective; coordinating planning time may be a challenge for either or both teachers
- It may be best to focus in on only particular units of study at first and then to gradually expand to more curricular areas

Benefits

When using this approach, teachers:

- Integrate special education strategies into the general education curriculum
- Directly meet the needs of their diverse learners by incorporating co-teaching structures
- Work collaboratively in a unified delivery of the lesson

Taken from The Co-Teaching Book of Lists, by Katherine Perez. Copyright © 2012 by John Wiley & Sons, Inc.

List 2.11   Adapting Curriculum Approach

Taken from *The Co-Teaching Book of Lists*, by Katherine Perez. Copyright © 2012 by John Wiley & Sons, Inc.

- One teacher takes the lead in instructing the class and the other roams to make adaptations and modifications on the spot as needed
- Teachers can prepare a basic tool kit to use as needed and share with the students (the kit might contain highlighters, index cards, plastic sleeves for pages, markers, and sticky notes, for example)
- The roles of the teachers should be flexible in this approach
- The lead teacher does not always have to be the content area specialist
- The special education teacher should deliver whole-class instruction and the content specialist should roam and provide modifications to the lesson so that both teachers are perceived as vital to instruction in the classroom
- Can be integrated into other whole-class co-teaching approaches
- Co-planning is absolutely critical to the success of this model
- Teachers need to be prepared in advance with appropriate adaptations that are targeted to the specific objectives of the lesson

Benefits

When using this approach, one teacher addresses the instruction to a large group of students, while the other teacher:

- Focuses in on the learning areas of special needs students
- Assists with modifying curriculum
- Promotes student engagement

List 2.12   Learning Styles Approach

- Tuning into students' preferred learning styles is another way to deliver instruction through co-teaching
- Teachers need to informally assess and observe students to determine the channel or modality through which each learner processes information best; the primary modalities are visual, auditory, and kinesthetic (or tactile)
- Although most classroom instruction tends to be visual and auditory, students learn best through multiple modalities
- Special education students are primarily tactile-kinesthetic learners, so there is a gap between teaching and learning in most classrooms today
- Co-teachers can maximize the learning of all students in their classroom when they combine their expertise; for instance, one teacher may be more adept at providing hands-on application for learning, while the other teacher is better at using visual representations to assist the learners
- This approach provides a natural way to differentiate instruction and maximize learning

Benefits

When using this approach, teachers:

- Promote a multi-modality approach to instruction
- Keep struggling students on task and engaged
- Scaffold curriculum by utilizing a variety of learning modes

Taken from *The Co-Teaching Book of Lists*, by Katherine Perez. Copyright © 2012 by John Wiley & Sons, Inc.

List 2.13   Checking in: Applying the Approaches

Read the classroom snapshot scenarios below. Using what you have learned about shared instruction and the co-teaching models described so far, determine which approach is demonstrated by the classroom vignette. Put the number of the approach next to the appropriate classroom situation. A discussion guide for this activity appears in the Appendix.

1. Skill group teaching
2. Alternative teaching
3. Duet teaching
4. Station teaching
5. Parallel teaching

Snapshot 1

Let's prepare for our social studies class. There are twenty-eight students for our fifty-minute class period. We can each work with different groups daily and Mrs. Perry, our paraprofessional, will be with us two days per week for thirty minutes. First we need to assess our students to find out their background knowledge on the Civil War and determine their interests. This will help us decide how many groups to have, who will work with each group, how much time we will need to work with them, and the outcomes and products they will produce.

Snapshot 2

In reading class today, let's set up three stations to address our students' different readiness levels. One station will do a character attribute map from our story, another station will do a feature analysis chart to compare the characters, and the third station will draw pictures of the main characters and make a flipbook listing their key characteristics. A fourth group will work independently on a word sort using the key vocabulary of the lesson.

Snapshot 3

Our new science unit on rocks and minerals seems to be perplexing for several of our students. Let's have one of us reteach the main concepts to the whole class and review the key points, then form groups of four students and jigsaw the reading. They will meet with their expert groups and then reteach main ideas to their home group. In this way, we can monitor their learning better. One of us can work with our target students in a small group while the lesson is going on.

Snapshot 4

I think our students would understand literature circles better in smaller groups, so they can talk more informally and try on the different roles with fewer students. Let's divide the class, work in different parts of the room, and each take a group. That way we can answer questions more readily and observe them better. This will also give the students more opportunities to interact with each other.

Snapshot 5

Why are fractions so difficult for students to understand? We clearly have students at different readiness levels here. Some students still need the manipulatives of fraction pizzas. Others are ready to start adding and dividing fractions. Some need extra help with word problems in fractions. Our advance learners are beginning to learn division of fractions. I will work with the small group using manipulatives, and you can move ahead with the larger group on fraction computation.

List 2.14   Co-Teaching Approaches: An Action Plan

Teachers: _____

Model	We'll try this one . . .	We tried it and liked it!	We tried and will pass . . .
Lead and Support			
Duet			
Speak and Add or Chart			
Skills Groups			
Learning Style			
Station Teaching			
Parallel Teaching			
Adapting			
Complementary			

List 2.15   Applying the Models: Develop and Do

What Would It Look Like in Practice?

Using the lesson objective given here, choose a co-teaching model that you could use and sketch out a lesson plan.

Lesson objective: students will be able to identify relevant questions for inquiry about the chapter.

Time	Activity	Materials	Person Responsible

Chapter 3

Where Do You Start?

List 3.1   First Steps for Beginning the Co-Teaching Experience

Many things need to be considered when beginning a co-teaching partnership: it is a multifaceted process of integrating teaching and planning effectively. Listed here are the first steps.

Get a Commitment of Support from Your Administrator

- Ensure that there is schoolwide support for co-teaching at your site
- Administrative support is essential for co-teaching success
- Create a special education master schedule first and allow special education students to schedule their classes before the general education master schedule; this ensures the availability of special education teachers and appropriate placement of students according to their specific needs and their IEPs

From an Administrator's Perspective: Prepare Your Teachers' Professional Development Planning

- Conduct a needs assessment for the entire staff about issues of concern for the co-teaching process
- Prepare a schedule for initial professional development and ongoing coaching and support throughout the year
- Hire an effective consultant who will customize the type of training to meet the needs of your staff
- Provide incentives so that general and special education teachers attend together
- Co-teachers need to plan for their own professional growth on an ongoing basis for continuation, extension, and possible changes in the program

List 3.2   Second Steps

- Define co-teaching as a team
- Consider the benefits and analyze the challenges carefully
- Assess your students' needs and your teaching styles
- Review various models and the content to be taught
- Clarify roles and responsibilities
- Develop procedures and routines
- Communicate, communicate, communicate!
- Start small! In the beginning, teach only one or two lessons
- Meet and debrief the experience
- Plan next steps together

Grouping for the Co-Taught Classroom

- Create a heterogeneous grouping of students for the co-taught classroom
- The proportion of special education students should not exceed 30 percent of the total number of students in any one class—depending on the students' needs and their IEPs
- Consider the nature of the general education students to maintain a positive mix in the co-taught classroom; too many "at-risk" general education students can prove problematic for student success, due to a lack of proper role models and escalated behavior management issues

Selecting a Co-Teaching Partner

- Be sure to select a partner who is willing to co-teach and is enthusiastic about the process
- Assess and make a list of each teacher's strengths and styles of teaching
- Share expectations and keep communication open
- Agree on a behavior management system
- Determine which students will be in the classes
- Inform other teachers, counselors, specialists, parents, and support staff
- Keep student success and mutual professional growth as priorities
- Allow plenty of time for program planning: what, how, when, and other big-picture questions

Select a Teaming Model to Use in the Co-Taught Classroom

- Review pros and cons of each approach and base your decision on the needs of the students and the content to be covered as well as the teaching styles of the teachers involved
- Whatever approach is selected, strive for equity between the two teachers in the classroom; it is important that the special educator has an active role

- Although special education teachers are primarily responsible for encouraging special education students to reach their IEP goals, they can also be a valuable resource for all of the students in the general education classroom
- Keep in mind that there is no one right way to approach co-teaching; the approaches may be changed as the relationship evolves, because co-teaching is a learning experience and can be used in alternative ways

List 3.3   Preparing for Co-Teaching: A Checklist to Review

Getting started in a co-teaching relationship is like starting over again from the beginning with each new partnership and program. You need to be clear about your goals so that you can communicate your desired outcomes with your administrator and your teaching partner. Involving and informing parents and the students are important in this process as well.

Planning Time

- When can we meet on a regular basis?
- Who will take primary responsibility for planning?
- When planning for a unit over time, is there another time when we can meet for additional planning?

Shared Teaching Responsibilities

- Who will determine curriculum focus?
- Who will plan the lessons?
- How can we both teach the lessons?
- Who will determine the unit objectives and important concepts?
- How will we determine learning strategies and modifications necessary for meeting individual students' needs?
- How will we develop support activities?
- How will the special education placement (IEP scheduling and identification) be maintained?
- Who will assess and grade assignments? How will we develop this process?

Preparing the Classroom

- How will we create a classroom environment that is inclusive of both teachers and all learners?
- How will we create greater equity in the classroom—among the students and ourselves as a team?

Keys to Classroom Management

- What are our rules or expectations in regard to student behavior?
- How should we acknowledge and reinforce desired and positive behaviors?
- How will we respond to infractions?
- What kind of consequences will we use?

Setting

- How will we set up the physical classroom space to accommodate a variety of co-teaching approaches?
- How conducive is the classroom space to support flexible grouping of the students?

The Co-Teaching Book of Lists

- How will we make sure that we each have our own space in the classroom?
- Is there any flexibility of the space needed? Are we able to utilize other space in the building?

Classroom Routines

- Meet and agree upon important classroom procedures and routines:
  - Pencil sharpening
  - Answering questions (hand raising)
  - Use of the restroom
  - Turning in homework
  - Distributing supplies
  - Positive reinforcement system
  - Passing out papers
  - Transitions between activities and groups

Noise

- Talk about different acceptable noise levels for different situations
- What is your tolerance level for noise in the classroom?
- Is there a signal when all is quiet and all eyes and ears are focused on teachers?

Discipline

- Determine classroom norms or conditions needed to work together (and involve the students in this process)
- Discuss acceptable limits of behavior with students
- Establish a clearly defined system of rewards and consequences
- Discuss who will be responsible for the behavior of certain students on a consistent basis

IEP Issues

- How will students' goals and objectives be communicated?
- How should these goals be addressed and monitored in the classroom?
- How will students' progress be monitored, and who will be responsible?

Accommodations and Modifications

- What specific modifications can we agree on for specific students?
- Who will implement them?
- How will we monitor this process?
- To what extent will the modifications be used with general education students who are also struggling?
- Should grades be adjusted because of modifications?

Grading Issues

- How will we grade homework?
- What are the issues about grading in-class assignments?
- Who is responsible for grading tests and quizzes?
- What grading system should we use?
- How will we monitor ongoing student progress?
- How can we develop rubrics for certain assignments?
- What district policies regarding grading should we take into account in making our decisions?

Obstacles

- What do you perceive as the biggest challenges that we face in this process?
- What are some ways that we can overcome them?
- What of our pet peeves should we be aware of in this classroom? What are the students' main pet peeves to keep in mind?

Communication

- What procedures will help us communicate and maintain a good working relationship?
- How will we communicate with parents? Students? Administration?
- How will we handle our communication needs with each other?

Taken from *The Co-Teaching Book of Lists*, by Katherine Perez. Copyright © 2012 by John Wiley & Sons, Inc.

List 3.4   Preparing to Teach Together

In terms of up-front planning, you need to designate a specific time to sit down with your co-teacher and discuss the pointers for planning described in this chapter. You might have the opportunity to choose your co-teaching partner. However, even when you don't have a choice, it's best to invite your colleague into the partnership and collaborate from the start. Following are some questions to help start the conversation.

Time Considerations

- How much time do we need for planning?
- When will we make the time to plan?
- What should we prepare in advance for the planning meeting?
- Should we establish an agenda format to use? Can we schedule this time on a regular basis?
- How will we most effectively use our time together?
- How can we best use our planning time to address the needs of all of our students?

Teaching Considerations

- How do we determine the content to be taught?
- How will we analyze students' needs?
- How will we differentiate the content, process, and product for *all* students?
- Will we use anchor activities, choice boards, tiering, curriculum compacting, mapping, and state standards to focus on the most critical content?
- Who will plan for what?
- How will we decide on instructional options?
- How will we make sure that special education students are able to complete assignments? Which modifications will we decide to use?
- How will we decide who teaches what?
- When will the special education teacher intervene with the special education students? Other students? Both?
- Who will make adaptations for testing and grading?
- How will we utilize our strengths and teaching styles in the classroom to maximize the advantages for the students?
- How will we present the content?
- How will we work with a paraprofessional? What will his or her role be?
- Should we rotate responsibilities on a regular basis?
- How will we evaluate the effectiveness of our program? How will we provide each other with appropriate feedback?

Management Issues

- What are the classroom expectations, procedures, and routines for students and co-teachers?

- How are these expectations communicated to the students? How do students participate in this process?
- What is our plan for classroom management?
- Which essential class rules are most important to us?
- Which procedures and routines will be most effective to implement?
- How do we plan to support positive behavior?
- How do we plan to deal with unacceptable behavior?
- What steps will we take to ensure consistency in classroom management?
- What will we tolerate in the classroom? What are our limits?
- Are our classroom management styles very different, or do we share common goals?

Process and Logistics

- How do we explain the co-teaching arrangement to the students?
- What procedures will we start with?
- How do we explain the co-teaching process to parents?
- How will the room be arranged?
- How will we accommodate space for flexible grouping patterns?
- How will the classroom space be shared?

List 3.5   Co-Teaching Planning Pointers

How Many Students Should Be in a Co-Taught Classroom?

- Maintain high standards for all learners while making accommodations for those who need them
- Look at the ratio of special education and general education students—too many special needs students can lead to a more challenging teaching situation
- Review student progress regularly
- Decide as a team on the composition of the classes and consider the number of at-risk learners and students with behavior disorders in determining the mix

How Do You Balance the Teaching Responsibilities?

- Start small, especially if co-teaching is a new approach in the school
- Remember that careful planning and lots of time are needed to learn how to collaborate effectively
- If special education teachers become specialists in a certain content area, utilize their skills in that content area for co-teaching
- Arrange for reteaching as needed
- Consider the special education teacher's caseload and overall responsibilities as you design the schedule
- Remember to factor in the general educator's other responsibilities, such as testing, meetings, and consulting
- Provide feedback and reinforce each other on an ongoing basis

How Often Should the Co-Teacher Be in the Classroom?

- When possible, daily contact is the most effective use of co-teaching time
- Modifications and adaptations should be shared and continued on an ongoing basis
- Intermittent arrangements need to be discussed and agreed on in advance

How Shall We Plan When There Is a Substitute Teacher?

- Make sure your substitute teacher plans include an explanation of the co-teaching approach that you use
- Ask the sub to consult with the other co-teacher in the room
- If the co-teacher is taking the lead for instruction that day, make sure there are clearly delineated duties for the sub to complete

What Are Some Obstacles to the Effectiveness of Co-Teaching?

- Lack of clearly defined roles and responsibilities
- Separating special education students from the whole class
- Lack of shared understanding about co-teaching or insufficient desire to make it work
- Placing too many special education students in one class

- Insufficient time for teachers to plan together
- Lack of time to debrief lessons
- Best teaching practices not being used
- Teaching responsibilities not shared

Source: Adapted from M. Friend and L. Cook, *Interactions: Collaboration Skills for School Professionals,* 4th ed. (Boston: Allyn & Bacon, 2003).

List 3.6   Ongoing Implementation

Once co-teaching is implemented, both the general education teacher and the special education teacher need to:

- Review effectiveness of the classroom management system
- Clearly communicate expectations with each other
- Collaborate on lesson planning and delivery of instruction
- Jointly evaluate the progress of students and of the co-teaching process, then decide on appropriate program modifications
- Plan for regularly scheduled reflection meetings
- Review student progress
- Arrange for reteaching as needed
- Evaluate tests, projects, and summative and formative assessment

List 3.7   Co-Planning Tips and Tricks

1. Set up a definite time to meet for planning and stick to it. Co-teaching teams should have a minimum of sixty minutes per week to plan.

2. Design the sequence of the unit in advance and place the benchmark lessons on a calendar. Then focus in on specific lessons that need more intense collaborative planning to make co-teaching more successful (duet or parallel teaching).

3. Be sure to vary your co-teaching approaches in accordance with the needs of your students and the content to be taught.

4. Use the curriculum content as the guiding force that determines what co-teaching approaches will maximize the learning for the lesson.

5. Be sure to schedule your co-planning time before anything else—and stick to it!

6. Preview upcoming curriculum content—write down resources, needs, activities, and student concerns.

7. Get mentally ready for the planning session—be flexible, open to new ideas, and prepared to contribute.

8. Don't start from scratch—come to the meeting with ideas, projects, products, and outcomes that you have prepared in advance. Better yet, e-mail or share your ideas with each other prior to the meeting to maximize your time together.

9. Try to plan two to three weeks in advance for a smoother and more integrated sequence. These plans can be adjusted at your weekly meetings as needed.

10. Remember: if you don't co-plan, you can't co-teach.

11. Deliver your lessons and reflect on their effectiveness, and provide feedback to each other.

12. Evaluate instructional effectiveness in accordance with student performance and assessment.

List 3.8   Maximizing Lesson Planning Time

Develop an instructional routine for each subject area time block. For example, a writer's workshop might look like this:

- First fifteen minutes: whole-group focus lesson
- Remaining thirty to forty-five minutes: individual, pair, and small-group work
- Guided writing with teacher(s)

Another example is a math block:

- First ten minutes: math warm-up activity with whole class
- Remaining thirty to forty-five minutes: small-group work or station teaching
- Independent seat work, with teacher reinforcing concepts with small groups

Be prepared for the planning meetings; agree on materials to collect ahead of time and prepare ideas for lessons

To plan a unit, decide on standards, essential learning, focus ideas, assessment process, and the timeline of the unit in the initial session; in subsequent sessions you can fine-tune the learning activities, grouping, and adaptations according to the needs of your students

Rotate the responsibility for making the detailed lesson plans and preparing the necessary materials after the main focus ideas and assessment process have been developed

Divide and conquer: sometimes it is easier for one teacher to plan the group lesson for a specific subject area like science, history, English, or math while the other teacher prepares the adaptations or alternative lessons for targeted students; each co-teacher plans for at least one primary content area, then they rotate that responsibility

Plan a minimum of a week at a time, then adjust the lesson plans as the week progresses according to the responses of the students

List 3.9   Co-Teaching Weekly Planning Guide

Planning for the week of _____

In the Classroom

Who is responsible for . . . ?

- Greeting the students as they enter the room
- Deciding on bell work and facilitating it
- Taking attendance
- Starting the class
- Distributing assignments, materials, books, and so forth
- Reviewing material previously taught
- Designing and delivering an "activator" activity
- Preteaching key vocabulary words
- Preteaching new concepts
- Reteaching key concepts as needed
- Practice and apply activity
- Reflection: summarizer activity
- Next steps: previewing learning for the next class
- Record keeping: to facilitate future planning

Preparation Considerations

- Select teaching objectives and outcomes
- Decide on the most effective ways to present the material to achieve your objectives
- Discuss how time can be used most effectively
- Decide on teaching and learning strategies for engagement
- Create graphic organizers to support instruction
- Decide on any modifications and accommodations needed for certain students
- Develop ideas for differentiating the content, process, and products for the lesson
- Discuss flexible grouping ideas based on student needs
- Create study guides and advance organizers
- Create practice sheets for reinforcement of key concepts
- Develop appropriate assessment tools that match instruction

Ongoing Issues

Both teachers in the co-teaching partnership should accomplish these ongoing tasks:

- Monitor and plan for daily classroom activities and adjust as necessary
- Meet weekly for management conferences
- Monitor progress of students
- Complete necessary paperwork and record keeping
- Provide support with curriculum adaptations as needed

Where Do You Start?

List 3.10   Practical Planning Pointers

Having time to plan is essential to a co-teaching program. If your school does not provide planning time, try some of the following options:

- Use time before school, after school, or during lunchtime to meet and plan, and remember—the goal is to make your job easier and your program more successful
- Try to arrange for a substitute for a half day per week to provide some collaborative time together; some schools hire permanent substitutes for co-teaching planning coverage
- Have parents or community members volunteer, or contact your local PTA for volunteers, to oversee your class while you plan with your co-teacher; or utilize the skills of a student teacher from a local university to oversee your class; because of liability issues, you will need to do the co-planning in the classroom
- Investigate whether stipends are available for compensation to plan beyond your contractual day
- Ask your principal to provide time in the faculty meeting agenda for co-planning
- When you have a special education teacher co-teaching with more than one general education teacher, leave the class period fifteen minutes early one day per week to work on a planning schedule while the content area teacher has a prep period (for instance, during first period Susan, a special education teacher, leaves her class fifteen minutes early to plan with Marcia, the general education teacher she works with during fourth period, because she has a prep period at that time)
- Substitute teachers may have free blocks of time during the day when the teacher they are subbing for has a prep period; schedule the sub during that time to cover your class so that you can work with your co-teacher
- When information must be shared before the next school day, set up a phone call or e-mail exchange that evening with your partner
- If the general education teacher can give the special education teacher copies of lesson plans, quizzes, and projects in advance, the special educator can come to class or planning time prepared to discuss modification options for specific targeted students
- Sharing lesson plans in advance is helpful, and if you use the Track Changes feature in Microsoft Word you can easily keep track of comments from both partners
- Ongoing sharing of assessment results and grading is critical for greater participation in the co-teaching process; these can be placed in the special educator's mailbox in advance for review before the planning meeting

The Co-Teaching Book of Lists

List 3.11   Planning a Co-Taught Unit

Title of Unit _____

Duration of Unit _____

Standards Addressed _____

Main Topics in the Unit

When this unit is finished, what are the essential ideas that students should know and understand? What will they be able to do?

What are the most important key vocabulary words that students need to know?

What background knowledge do students need in order to understand the main concepts of the unit?

What skills are required for students to be successful in this unit?

What are the major assignments in the unit? How can these be differentiated to maximize student strengths?

How will student learning be assessed?

Where will differentiation of content, process, and products be needed?

How will we share teaching responsibilities?

List 3.12   Co-Teaching Planning Form

Student	Grade
Leaning style	Multiple intelligence
Interests	
Strengths	Challenges
Notes and reminders:	
Areas of concern:	

Class Activity	Student Activity	Goals Met	Supports Needed

List 3.13   Reviewing the Co-Planning Process

Review (Ten to Fifteen Minutes)

- Think about your teaching *and* student performance
- What worked well?
- What did not work well?
- What should we do about it?

Plan Next Week's Lessons (Twenty-Five to Thirty Minutes)

- Discuss big-picture issues first
- Discuss content
- Plan content delivery
- Consider various approaches to output and input
- Design practice activities
- Plan for individual and small-group evaluation

Assign Responsibilities (Twenty Minutes)

- Identify needed responsibilities
- Clarify teaching roles and responsibilities
- Write out plans for all involved

Ongoing Evaluation

- Debrief daily
- Give praise for your efforts together
- Provide constructive feedback of each week's activities objectively
- Be honest and open with each other
- Use problem-solving strategies
- Revisit roles and responsibilities on a regular basis

Review Efficient Co-Planning Checklist

- Be prepared
- Be on time
- Use an agenda
- Plan at a convenient and consistent time
- Plan in a quiet place without distractions whenever possible
- Monitor your time
- Stay focused on planning
- Record the plan
- Review frequently

List 3.14   Co-Teaching Roles and Responsibilities

Conditions of Clarity

- Each member needs to be aware of the task and outcomes to focus on
- Roles and responsibilities need to be flexible and adjusted for the task, the students, and the lessons
- Distribution of responsibilities should be equitable
- Teachers should share the classroom and the instruction

Ponder the Possibilities

- Have you distributed the responsibilities fairly?
- Have you taken into account the needs of the students and the expertise of the teachers?
- Have you described the tasks thoroughly?
- Have you planned for clear outcomes?
- Have you developed measurable goals?

List 3.15   Determining Roles and Responsibilities

Discuss the following roles and responsibilities in order to clarify expectations and to facilitate planning

Who will be responsible for . . . ? (if responsibility is shared, check more than one box)	General Educator	Special Educator	Paraprofessional	Other
Planning content area instruction and lessons Determining goals and objectives				
Writing lesson plans Organizing instructional materials				
Insuring that lesson plans address necessary student accommodations and modifications that are aligned with IEP objectives				
Developing assignments and classroom activities to achieve goals				
Accommodating or modifying assignments and classroom activities				
Preparing supplemental materials when needed Developing a classroom management plan Taking care of daily routines				
Collecting data on student performance Establishing evaluation procedures and grading				
Designing preteaching and/or reteaching plans for follow-up Developing and modifying homework as needed				

Who will be responsible for...? (if responsibility is shared, check more than one box)	General Educator	Special Educator	Paraprofessional	Other
Teaching specific study skills and/or compensatory learning strategies				
Designing behavior intervention or management programs for specific target students				
Designing formative and summative assessments				
Developing test accommodations or modifications as needed				
Communicating with parents Participating in conferences				
Communicating with grade-level or departmental colleagues Communicating with administrator about program and progress				
Maintaining IEP data on students' goals and objectives Preparing interim reports as needed				

List 3.16   Role Clarity

After carefully reviewing the Determining Roles and Responsibilities checklist in List 3.15, it is important to have a conversation with your co-teacher about your teaching philosophies and styles, as well as the expectations you have of each other.

Expectations of the Special Educator

It is expected that the special educator will:

- Provide modified work for students in advance if he or she is not in class
- Fully participate in the day-to-day logistics of classroom maintenance (assignments, attendance, homework, and so on)
- Evaluate student work in a shared capacity
- Plan and participate in parent conferences
- Work as an active classroom member with parity to the general education teacher

Expectations of the General Educator

It is expected that the general educator will:

- Take an active role in the IEP process, including developing objectives and evaluating attainment of goals
- Assist in making accommodations for students with special needs
- Understand that the special educator has other responsibilities in other classrooms in addition to this one
- Share the delivery of instruction for students with special needs
- Adhere to the instructional schedule and be consistent
- Notify the special educator of any changes in scheduling

List 3.17   Sample Co-Teaching Duties

Please note: *The following are examples only. These responsibilities need to be very fluid and agreed on by the teachers involved. They may be modified depending on the needs of the students and/or the content of the lessons.*

General Education Teacher

- Collaborates with entire team including students, paraprofessionals and students
- Shares the planning of daily lessons, activities, assignments, and assessments with the special education teacher
- Develops the curriculum plan, classroom management plan, classroom layout, and materials in collaboration with the co-teacher
- Oversees the responsibilities of the paraprofessional in classroom routines
- Works in tandem with the special educator in developing curriculum modifications and assessment issues
- Implements adaptations and modifications that are recommended by the goals and objectives of the IEP
- Considers enrichment opportunities for all students to extend and reinforce concepts

Special Education Teacher

- Recommends instructional strategies to meet the needs of all of the students
- Teaches specific target skills and reteaches as necessary for certain students
- Provides recommendations for curriculum modifications and interventions for students regarding materials, content, products, and behavior plans
- Develops classroom management policy with the general education teacher
- Collaborates with the general education teacher to develop lesson plans for the whole class, small groups, and individualized instruction as appropriate
- Works directly with students as a whole class, with small groups, or with individuals
- Modifies general education materials, assessment procedures, and assignments as necessary
- Develops IEP goals and objectives with general educator's input

Paraprofessional

- Implements instructional modifications developed by the co-teaching team
- Follows classroom policies and procedures developed by the classroom teachers
- Provides assistance for all students

- Facilitates learning opportunities for individual students and small groups as planned by the teacher or specialist
- Reteaches specific skills as needed by target students
- Implements IEP modifications under the guidance of the general and special educators
- Charts progress of students

List 3.18   Introducing the Co-Teaching Team

From the onset it is important that you do not introduce yourselves to the students as the "special education teacher" and the "general education teacher." These labels may cause stigma, especially for those students with special needs in the class. They give students the false impression that one teacher is the "real" teacher and the other teacher works only with students with disabilities.

- Introduce one teacher as the content area specialist and the other one as the learning strategies specialist
- Place *both* your names on the classroom door in the hallway
- Ask other co-teaching teams to avoid all labels and simply introduce themselves as the teachers of the classroom
- Emphasize the aspect of teamwork and explain that both of you will be working with small groups, large groups, and individuals

List 3.19   Who Does What in a Co-Taught Classroom?

The following list of possible roles and responsibilities when planning lessons in the co-taught classroom is meant to be used as a guide only. Optional, interchangeable duties are also offered here. This list should be considered after a thorough discussion of roles and responsibilities of each teacher and how these responsibilities might change depending on the co-teaching approach used.

Co-Teacher #1 Is Teaching a Lesson to the Whole Class

Co-teacher #2 is:

- Presenting content in a different way, developing visuals and posters to reinforce concepts
- Preparing a digital slide presentation of key ideas
- Creating handouts and worksheets to extend and review material of lesson
- Checking for understanding by roaming around classroom
- Observing student responses and planning for follow-up
- Repeating or clarifying information to students
- Doing independent work for task mastery
- Completing behavior documentation plans
- Conducting action research and data collection using student work samples
- Ensuring that students have necessary accommodations for lesson mastery
- Using proximity and position control for classroom management
- Developing ideas for enrichment of instructional objectives
- Collecting homework and using the information gleaned to help form targeted small-group instruction
- Repeating or clarifying difficult concepts for some students

Co-Teacher #1 Is Taking Attendance

Co-teacher #2 is:

- Reviewing material taught the previous day
- Organizing materials to be used for instruction
- Providing a preview activity to activate prior knowledge of upcoming lesson
- Checking student work for completion

Co-Teacher #1 Is Collecting Homework

Co-teacher #2 is:

- Introducing a study skill to the class
- Writing learning objectives on the board
- Conducting an activator lesson to engage student in learning
- Doing a connector activity to relate the key concepts of the previous day's lesson

Taken from *The Co-Teaching Book of Lists*, by Katherine Perez. Copyright © 2012 by John Wiley & Sons, Inc.

Co-Teacher #1 Is Passing Out Handouts

Co-teacher #2 is:

- Providing specific directions for the assignment both visually and verbally
- Modeling the first problem or idea of the lesson on the board
- Eliciting questions about the assignment
- Engaging students in a pair-share on what they know about the topic and questions they have
- Charting responses from the students

Co-Teacher #1 Is Giving Directions Orally

Co-teacher #2 is:

- Providing visual reinforcement with directions on the board or overhead
- Repeating and clarifying confusing concepts
- Rephrasing questions
- Providing a graphic organizer of the lesson with key concepts
- Preparing vocabulary lists to teach before reading

Co-Teacher #1 Is Explaining New Content for the Lesson

Co-teacher #2 is:

- Modeling the new concept using manipulatives
- Modeling a note-taking strategy on the overhead
- Engaging the students in a role-play
- Facilitating a pair-share activity using higher-order thinking skills
- Charting the key concepts on the board
- Prompting students to summarize
- Reteaching skill to select students

Co-Teacher #1 Is Administering a Test with a Group of Students

Co-teacher #2 is:

- Reading the test out loud with extended time for a target group of students
- Transcribing answers to prompts from specific students
- Paraphrasing test questions and clarifying issues for some students
- Modeling the main concepts of the assessment to a group of students

Co-Teacher #1 Is Facilitating an Independent Activity

Co-teacher #2 is:

- Roaming around the classroom checking for understanding
- Implementing accommodations and modifications as interventions to the assignment given
- Facilitating other students doing reciprocal teaching in small groups

Co-Teacher #1 Is Facilitating a Learning Center

Co-teacher #2 is:

- Facilitating another small group at a learning center
- Explaining the use of learning stations for independent work with accelerated students

Co-Teacher #1 Is Preteaching or Reteaching a Lesson with a Small Group of Students

Co-teacher #2 is:

- Monitoring a large group and facilitating their completion of an assignment
- Coordinating an enrichment activity for a group of students who do not need reteaching of the concept
- Facilitating a group project that engages the learners to demonstrate their understanding of the lesson

Co-Teacher #1 Is Creating Standards-Based Lesson Plans for a Particular Unit

Co-teacher #2 is:

- Providing suggestions for modifications to the content, process, and products of the unit to accommodate diverse learner needs
- Sharing in the planning of the unit and paying particular attention to attainment of IEP goals for specific students

List 3.20　Communication Issues and Co-Teaching

Work together with your co-teacher by discussing these prompts to foster more positive communication.

Getting to Know You: Paired Interviews

- Capture your images of exemplary co-teaching. Draw an image, picture, or symbol of what co-teaching means to you. Share your drawing with your partner and explain how it symbolizes co-teaching for you.
- Share your dreams with your partner—what does co-teaching look like at its best?
- What values do you both embrace?
- What are your hopes for this co-teaching process?
  - For your students?
  - For yourselves?
- What specific talents do you bring to this co-teaching partnership?
- Combining our strengths will enable us to . . .
- What do you think will "push my buttons" about your behavior?
- What do you value most about teaching?
- What are the biggest obstacles and challenges we face?
- How are we going to avoid some of the pitfalls?

List 3.21   Conversation Starters

Why Are We Doing This?

- What is our purpose in co-teaching?
- What influences our decisions?
- What targeted outcomes do we have for our students?

How Will We Communicate with Each Other?

- How will we ensure regular and ongoing communication with each other?
- How will we address our communication needs with each other?
- What is the best way to share the responsibility of communication equally?
- How will we communicate with the parents of our special education students? General education students?
- Who will communicate with parents about daily routines, unusual situations, and other issues?
- What do we need to know about each other?

What Does the Ideal Co-Teaching Situation Look Like?

- What will you be doing?
- What will I be doing?
- What will the students be doing?
- How might we be working together?
- What am I looking forward to in this co-teaching relationship?
- What is the most important thing in our co-teaching relationship?

How Will We Determine Our Success?

- What are our expectations of each other?
- What will our students be doing when they are successful?
- How will we know we are successful? What are some of the indicators?
- What do I need to do in order to work more effectively with you in the classroom?
- What will we do to continue to make progress?

What Contributions Do We Each Make to Co-Teaching?

- What strengths or talents do I bring to this co-teaching relationship?
- Which elements of my teaching style are most important to me?
- What do I hope to learn and gain from this co-teaching process?
- What are my nonnegotiables?
- How do we each react to unexpected changes to our plans?
- What pet peeves will we need to tell each other about?

Taken from *The Co-Teaching Book of Lists*, by Katherine Perez. Copyright © 2012 by John Wiley & Sons, Inc.

The Co-Teaching Book of Lists

What Are My Values and Beliefs as a Teacher?

- What do I hope to accomplish with our students? Our program?
- What are my goals as a teacher?
- How do I learn best?
- What are my beliefs about how students learn best?
- How do I view the change process?
- How flexible am I about routines and procedures in the classroom?

How Can We Establish Greater Parity in Our Co-Teaching Relationship?

- How should we share the roles and distribute the functions in the classroom?
- What will we do to promote greater parity in the classroom from the beginning?
- When one of us wants to share a new idea, should we present it in writing first so that there's time to process, or just talk about it?
- How will we alternate responsibilities for facilitating small and large groups?

What Are the Concerns or Potential Conflicts in Our Co-Teaching Relationship?

- How should we handle conflict or issues with each other to preserve the harmony of our relationship?
- What might help us move forward if we get stuck?
- What is the best way to approach our challenges and fears?
- What can I absolutely not tolerate in my co-teacher?
- How should we divide the workload?
- How should we give and receive feedback in order to avoid conflict?

What Are Our Students Like?

- How do we reach the individual needs of all of our diverse learners?
- What are our students' strengths and challenges?
- How are they alike? How are they different?
- How will we group our students?
- How can we foster a strong sense of community in our class?
- In what ways can we differentiate our instruction so that all students can succeed?

List 3.22   Communication Tips and Techniques

Here are several techniques to help you improve your communication skills with your co-teacher:

- Be positive! When working together, keep that can-do attitude.
- Understand that people value being heard. Practice active listening strategies such as:
  - "Tell me more about your concern."
  - "What is it about _____ that concerns you?"
- Instead of focusing on what's wrong with your teaming situation, look for what is working between you
- Do unexpected nice things for each other, like:
  - "I'll make copies of that for you after school."
  - Bring your partner treats unexpectedly
  - Take time out for appreciation time—share good things that are happening
  - Provide positive feedback
- Look for the common ground and the things you share in common, instead of the differences
- Share your intentions and desired outcomes for an assignment or lesson so that you will not be misunderstood
- If you do not know the answer to a question or dilemma that is presented to you, admit it; offer to take time to find out more or work together to find a solution
- Seek to understand before trying to be understood—focus on your partner's needs
- Try to see your partner's perspective—reframe any negative self-talk
- Check on your emotions; don't try to solve a challenging issue until you have had time to calm down, so that you will not say or do something that is divisive in your partnership
- Try using I-statements when responding to your co-teacher:
  - "When you _____, I feel _____, because _____."
- Keep the focus on *your* feelings
- Acknowledge your partner through positive body language, nodding, or verbal response
- Try asking for more specific information to clarify the situation
- Paraphrase or clarify what the person has said so that there will not be a misunderstanding
- Ask for elaboration to get more specific information
- Listen with the intention of understanding the other person's perspective

Taken from *The Co-Teaching Book of Lists*, by Katherine Perez. Copyright © 2012 by John Wiley & Sons, Inc.

The Co-Teaching Book of Lists

List 3.23   Collaboration Is the Key

When beginning the co-teaching process, the following ideas may be positive ways to start in order to foster greater collaboration and teamwork.

- Write instructions on the board, on a poster, or overhead while the other teacher speaks
- Schedule homework help sessions with students
- Intersperse questions through the lesson to greater clarify the content for more reticent students
- Use proximity techniques (get physically closer to students who may need extra help)
- Set up materials for station learning
- Provide additional examples or model concepts to be learned from the lesson
- Implement modifications to curriculum for target students
- Gather observational data about students' comprehension of the lesson and offer support where needed
- Stay involved! Don't recede to the sidelines.

List 3.24   Ways to Ease in a Special Educator as a Partner in the Classroom

Integrating co-teaching in your classroom does not occur overnight; however, you can take steps to ensure that both teachers achieve parity and equality of voice. Try some of these techniques to facilitate the process.

- Preteach key vocabulary, using kinesthetic and visual techniques as activating strategies
- Facilitate the daily warm-up or morning meeting to get the day started and to engage the students
- Carefully review curriculum to be covered, and model modifications for struggling students to assist them with note-taking, graphic organizers, and preparing for tests
- Help students connect new concepts to big ideas through a quick-write activity or partner-share technique
- Model a think-aloud strategy for an interactive reading lesson

List 3.25   A Blueprint for Collaborative Teaching

What are some of the things you need to think about before you start collaborating in the classroom? As you review this list with your co-teacher, use a check mark for the items that are currently in place. Enter a plus symbol for items that you need to develop or consider for your classroom.

- ❑ Review the essential elements of successful collaboration
- ❑ Share your goals for collaborative teaching, both for yourself and for the students
- ❑ Design ways to collaborate on monitoring and assessing students
- ❑ Decide how you will monitor your progress in collaboration
- ❑ Examine the factors in place for administrative support and determine whether more support is needed
- ❑ Identify your interpersonal teaching styles and the support you need from each other
- ❑ Discuss your beliefs about fairness in the classroom, student motivation, student engagement, and curriculum design
- ❑ Determine which instructional strategies are most comfortable for you
- ❑ Develop a design for teaching collaboratively in the classroom
- ❑ List the resources you will need to be successful
- ❑ Create a system for eliciting feedback from parents about the co-teaching process
- ❑ Design a discussion guide or process for eliciting and giving feedback to each other
- ❑ Set aside a time to meet with other collaborative teams at your school site or other sites to evaluate and provide other perspectives on collaboration

Taken from *The Co-Teaching Book of Lists*, by Katherine Perez. Copyright © 2012 by John Wiley & Sons, Inc.

Chapter 4

Where Do You Go? A Co-Teaching Road Map

List 4.1   Scheduling Considerations for Co-Teaching

Scheduling for co-teaching is a complex process. Effective scheduling may take years to work out in some cases. Be patient. Be flexible. Try different approaches. Learn from your mistakes.

A common question asked at the beginning stages of co-teaching is: How many students with special needs should be placed in the general education classroom to be served by a co-teaching model?

Here are some general considerations to ponder:

- Make sure that staff members are aware that scheduling takes time
- Instead of complaining about what is not working, have staff focus on problem-solving solutions
- Form a scheduling team with various stakeholders working together: special education, general education, administrator, counselor, and other support staff
- For the first year or two, start gradually: perhaps schedule some in-class support and retain a resource specialist program for target students
- Base student placement on individual student needs; refer to the special education teacher for assistance with these decisions
- In both elementary and secondary programs, consider the range of services available for the students at the *beginning* of the co-teaching program
- The more a schedule addresses the full range of services for students, the greater the chances that students' needs will be met effectively
- Be prepared for only partial successes in your program at first; remember to remain flexible, readjust, and use co-teaching to support the students with the greatest needs

Elementary Considerations

- Get the big picture first before you do class-by-class scheduling to identify situations where services would be most beneficial
- Schedules for special education teachers and paraprofessionals should have flexibility at the beginning of the year until all participating students are identified and placed
- Prioritize and develop the co-teaching schedule by grade levels first
- Determine how many students need self-contained services and schedule them together to maximize their support
- In designing the schedule, general education teachers may need to adjust the time period when they teach reading and math to accommodate students with special needs

Secondary Considerations

- Consider scheduling the special education teacher to a specific co-teaching team, grade level, or a specific content area
- Grouping the specialist's in-class services may be an advantage (for example, the special education teacher can work with the juniors during third-period math on

certain days and with the sophomore class on other days; teachers need to fine-tune the schedule according to the content and the needs of their students)

- Sometimes it is advantageous to schedule the special education teacher by the day of the week, in order to cover many subject areas and interface with different general education teachers; however, the targeted students with the greatest needs should receive specialized services on most of the days
- Make sure you allow time in your schedule for planning
- Students can be clustered in specific classrooms with collaborative teachers who are willing to accept the challenge
- Another option is to schedule the co-teaching experience to enhance and enrich specific units of instruction; then the special education teacher rotates to different classes to assist and support specific students for major assignments and projects

List 4.2   Effective Methods for Placing Students in a Co-Taught Classroom

- Choose student-teacher combinations carefully to avoid overloading certain general education classrooms

- Avoid placing special needs students in classrooms that already have several high-risk or emotionally disturbed students; you may need to handpick the students and the receiving teachers for specific situations

- Try to distribute the members of student cliques across different classrooms; these may be students who have been together in self-contained classes and have already developed certain negative behaviors

- Look at the prospective class combinations carefully to maximize the learning of all students, including matching the academic needs of advanced learners as well as those with disabilities

- Review and coordinate other services that special education students might need, including speech therapy, occupational therapy, and adaptive physical education; the specialists involved also need to be considered in designing the schedule

- Students with special needs should be placed first, before the master schedule is complete; this requires administrative support of the co-teaching program

List 4.3   Finding Time to Plan

When Are the Best Meeting Times for You?

Name _____

Please mark your first (1), second (2), and third (3) choices for possible meeting times.

	Mon	Tues	Wed	Thurs	Fri
8:00					
9:00					
10:00					
11:00					
12:00					
1:00					
2:00					
3:00					

List 4.4   Co-Teaching Daily Lesson Plans

General Educator _____

Special Educator _____

Date	What are you going to teach?	Which co-teaching approach will you use?	What are the specific tasks of both teachers?	What materials are needed?	How will you evaluate learning?	What kind of followup is needed? For which students?

The Co-Teaching Book of Lists

List 4.5 Expanding Planning Time for Co-Teaching

- Use staff development days for co-teachers to do more long-range planning
- Have two classes at the same grade level team up to release one teacher for planning with the special education teacher
- Use staff meeting time to discuss common co-teaching issues across grade levels
- Work with the administrator to treat co-planning time as a priority equal with other school committee work
- Find funds for substitute teachers to release teachers for planning; these funds might be obtained through grants, foundations, or parent-teacher organizations
- Try organizing a late arrival or early dismissal day with administrative support and use the time to work with colleagues; just adding fifteen or twenty minutes a day to the school day can easily make up this "borrowed" time and will provide a dedicated hour on the fifth day for planning
- Try to arrange planning time concurrent with current lunch or recess breaks to increase the time to plan together
- Have a special snack time after school or have breakfast together in the morning before school; partners can alternate bringing snacks to share
- Contact your local institution of higher education to offer continuing education credit for planning time outside of contractual hours
- Ask administration to offer incentives to help compensate teachers for planning on their own time outside the instructional day

List 4.6   Using Planning Time Effectively

- Try to plan for one week at a time (or longer segments if you are planning a unit that will last several weeks)
- Give the special education teacher the lesson plans a week in advance to allow him or her to develop necessary modifications to the core content
- Come prepared to plan, and have all the materials you think you will need ready
- One co-teacher can plan the group lesson about the content area while the other teacher plans accommodations and modifications
- Develop a set structure for your teaching time together in the classroom. The approach can change; however, certain components should be in place. Some ideas include:
  - Connect—warm-up or activator
  - Chunk—new information
  - Chew—process time
  - Check—do they understand?
  - Close—summarizer activity

First, Agree on a Lesson-Planning Approach

- Use standards-based planning
- Decide on the content to be learned
- Focus on the "big ideas"
- What are the most important elements for students to learn in this unit?
- Why is this information important? Establish the rationale:
  - What should the students know and be able to do as a result of this lesson?
  - What are the essential skills? What do you want the students to learn?
- *Assessment*—how will you know that the students have learned?
- *Learning activities*—what powerful learning strategies can you use and differentiate to meet the diverse needs of the students?
- *Reteaching*—what do you do when the students don't learn?

The Co-Teaching Book of Lists

List 4.7   Application: Putting Planning into Action

You have one hour to plan with your co-teacher. Where will you begin? What will you discuss? What are the essential outcomes of this planning time?

Planning notes:

_____

_____

_____

_____

_____

_____

_____

_____

_____

_____

_____

_____

_____

_____

_____

Outcomes:

_____

_____

_____

_____

_____

_____

_____

_____

List 4.8   Co-Planning Agenda Tips

Reflect on Previous Week

- How would you evaluate students' lesson mastery this past week?
- What worked well? What did not work well? Why?
- What are our learning opportunities moving forward?
- Which students need additional support?
- How can we reteach the content so that they can succeed?
- What can we do to improve our results?

Develop a Plan for the Next Week

You will need to decide on many facets of the instructional plan:

- Curriculum content: what is to be taught?
- Assessment process: what did students learn, and how are we going to measure it?
- Learning strategies and activities: how can we vary these for greater engagement?
- Instructional pacing: was it too fast or slow?
- Grouping: how can we diversify grouping patterns for the next week?
- Roles: which approach should we use for each lesson?

Adjust Instruction to Fit Student Needs

- Identify any students who may need more intensified instruction—what scaffolds to their learning can you create?
- Some students need greater emphasis on the big ideas, instead of attention to details, which they find distracting—what are the key ideas in this lesson or unit?
- Which support structures would make a difference for our target students, and why?
  - Individualized instruction
  - Station teaching
  - Learning contracts
  - Peer tutoring
  - Small-group work
  - Modified materials or assignments
- Do some students need the curriculum expanded and enriched to keep them engaged?

Determine Resources Needed and Decide on Responsibilities

- What additional materials and resources will be needed?
- How will we divide the responsibilities for preparing and teaching for next week?

The Co-Teaching Book of Lists

List 4.9   Procedures and Routines

Structures

It is necessary to clearly define and develop the details of the following structures prior to the planning meeting, so that procedures and routines can be established effectively:

- Co-teaching models/approaches
- Lesson plans
- Schedules
- Organizers
- Planning protocols and templates
- Space and logistical issues
- Flexible grouping

Establishing Procedures and Routines

Developing clearly defined procedures and routines will allow you to focus more on your co-teaching partnership and the success of your students. Procedures enable you to stay organized and to teach with a purpose in mind. The key to successful procedures and routines for teachers as well as students is to practice them every day.

Why Are Routines Important?

Routines help all students remember:

- How the class will begin (Will there be a warm-up? Bell work? Attendance?)
- Where to get and put away materials
- Record-keeping techniques for work accomplished
- How to transition between activities and move around the room without disrupting others
- How to use their time wisely
- What to do when they finish their task early
- How to keep track of the time and tasks accomplished
- What they should be doing according to the published schedule
- How to get assistance when the teacher is not available
- How the class will end (Will there be a reflection? A summarizer activity? Exit cards?)
- What they are responsible for and when it is due

Some Additional Procedures

- *Visual cues*
  - Use visual reminders to show students where to put their work
  - Use visual icons for steps at work stations

- Use visual coding strategy to connect with text using sticky notes (described in Chapter Nine, on instructional strategies)
- Create a color-coded graphic of the class schedule
- Use *sign language* and hand signals to attract students' attention (have students use sign language as well):
  - ''I need to use the restroom''
  - ''I have the answer''
  - ''Speak more quietly''
  - ''Time is up—turn in your work''
  - ''I need more time''
- *Task cards* with goals indicated:
  - Use with small groups or independent work
  - Time left to complete task
  - Reminders of various steps
  - Checkpoints for teachers
  - Steps to complete an activity or station
- *Transitions* between activities
  - Going to lunch
  - Lining up for recess
  - Switching classes
  - Transitioning between groups
  - Getting ready to go home
  - Putting away materials
  - Talking about progress—reflecting on the day

The Co-Teaching Book of Lists

List 4.10   Scheduling Co-Teaching

The scheduling process for co-teaching can be very challenging, especially with the multiple options at the secondary level. At the elementary level, the biggest challenge may arise from the lack of special education teachers needed at each grade level to ensure co-teaching throughout the school.

Another challenge is the requirement in many states of placing highly qualified teachers in every classroom. This mandate requires that special education teachers be highly qualified in each of the multiple content areas that they interface with through co-teaching.

Administrative support needs to ensure that co-taught classes are not disproportionately filled with students with special needs. The nature of the students' disabilities also needs to be considered: when too many students have more severe disabilities, co-teaching may become more difficult.

There is no specific data on the "ideal" percentage of students with disabilities in any one co-teaching classroom. It seems reasonable that proportion of 25 percent of students with special needs should be a maximum in a co-taught classroom.

Chapter 5

Collaboration: Working as a Team

List 5.1   What Is a Team?

Together

Everyone

Achieves

More

Very often, teams are formed just by gathering some people together and then hoping they will find a way to work together. However, teams are most effective when carefully designed and developed over time.

Team: an interdependent group of people that is formed and focused on the achievement of a task

Pieces of the Puzzle: Components of a Team

- Objectives and outcomes
- Clearly defined roles
- Organized structure
- Decision-making process
- Collaborative communication
- Positive climate
- Evaluation process

Teamwork is at the essence of a co-teaching relationship.

List 5.2   Characteristics of Co-Teaching Teams

Co-teaching teams need to provide coordinated services to students and agree to:

- Collaborate on common instructional goals for the classroom
- Share common core beliefs and values and validate their unique strengths and areas of expertise
- Have a shared language to discuss teaching and learning
- Strive for equality in the classroom and shared leadership roles
- Redistribute leadership roles and responsibilities as well as decision making and how the content will be presented
- Exchange their individual ideas and approaches openly despite difference in knowledge, skills, and experiences with their co-teacher
- Describe how they are going to share their individual expertise in the classroom
- Establish common goals and procedures to share their unique knowledge, skills, and resources
- Engage in cooperative interactions and promote interpersonal skills as well as individual accountability
- Encourage creative problem solving and foster social interactions by giving feedback to each other
- Decide on when and how often they will meet
- Monitor progress by checking in with each other regarding students' learning goals and which activities need to be modified
- Revisit the various co-teaching approaches on a regular basis to ensure that they are maximizing the expertise of both teachers

List 5.3 Forming an Effective Co-Teaching Team

The success of co-teaching programs depends entirely on the teacher team involved. In a strong, collaborative partnership, teachers need to ask themselves the following questions before they begin to work together:

- When will we have time to plan?
- How will we plan more effectively?
- How will the approach to co-teaching be determined?
- How will our roles be decided?
- How will we convey to students the equity that we maintain in the classroom?
- What will we communicate to students, parents, administrators, and others about our roles and our program?
- How will we communicate with parents, the principal, and with other specialists?
- How will grading and assessment be determined?
- How can we both be involved in the IEP process?
- What is most important to us in establishing procedures and routines for classroom management?
- How will we handle adverse behaviors in the classroom?
- What will we do for consistent positive reinforcement?
- What is most important for us to do in the classroom? What is least important?
- How will we develop lesson plans and keep records?
- What about the physical setup of the classroom?
- How can we support flexible grouping in the space we have?
- Will there be a teacher's desk that we share—or will we each have our own?
- How do we plan to work with all students and share the instruction?
- When will we build in time for reflection and adjustment?

List 5.4   Ingredients of Excellence for Your Co-Teaching Teams

Prioritize your co-teaching planning meetings as a "must do" on your weekly schedule. The best way to do this is by sharing the same prep period with your co-teacher.

Planning Pointers

- Be specific about the tasks to be accomplished
- Validate and utilize the strengths of both team members
- Be equitable in the distribution of duties—divide and conquer!
- Be flexible in the co-teaching approaches used and don't get stuck in a rut; tune into the students' needs and the outcomes of the lessons to decide which method works best

Collaborative Communication

- Decide how you will communicate during planning sessions and between sessions
- Create equity of voice in your conversations
- Use active listening skills and paraphrasing
- Record your ideas so that strategies, expectations, and outcomes are clearly delineated

Scheduling Issues

- Keep in mind the master schedule of the school—how does your schedule fit in?
- Be sure to consider the schedule of other specialists and support staff who might provide services for your students with special needs
- Make your schedule reasonable for both teachers; sometimes special education teachers need to work with more than one teacher during the day and week

Manage Physical Space in Classroom

- Make sure both teachers have adequate space for their materials and to meet with students
- Arrange students' desks for greater mobility
- Make space to allow for flexible grouping

Design a Communication Board

- Use this board to share information with each other, with students, and to exchange notes to parents
- This board can also be used for information updates, schedule changes, and last-minute details

Negotiate Decisions

- Keep in mind that you will not agree on everything
- Consensus building is a must
- Value differing perspectives; they will add more value to the co-teaching experience
- Respect each other
- Remain flexible
- Base your decisions on data, not feelings

List 5.5   Relationship Building Blocks

To build a stronger relationship between co-teachers, the following attributes need to be considered:

- Ability to swap positions at any time
- A shared common vision: listening, supporting, and believing in each other
- A committed belief that all students can learn and succeed
- Willingness to remove obstacles and problem-solve together
- Willingness to redistribute job functions and share responsibilities
- An acceptance of student differences and a commitment to do something about these differences
- Confidence in each other and your individual teaching styles
- Enjoying the process and taking each day as a new adventure
- Being flexible and adaptable to change
- Being able to defend one another
- Trusting and respecting each other
- Engaging in action research and data-driven decisions by analyzing student work samples
- Providing constructive feedback to each other on a regular basis

List 5.6   Team Preparation: What Do I Bring?

My professional strengths as a teacher are:

_____

_____

Personal qualities that inform my teaching are:

_____

_____

My teaching challenges are:

_____

_____

Areas of growth for me are:

_____

_____

My teaching style is (for example, creative, structured, traditional, or relaxed):

_____

_____

Three words to describe my classroom are:

_____

_____

What concerns me about my classroom is:

_____

_____

My classroom management style is:

_____

_____

My tolerance for noise levels is:

_____

_____

My technology skills are:

_____

_____

My greatest accomplishment in the classroom is:

_____

_____

My beliefs about teaching and learning are:

_____

_____

I am looking forward to co-teaching because:

_____

_____

My biggest challenge in co-teaching will be:

_____

_____

Co-teaching will be a success for me if:

_____

_____

Taken from *The Co-Teaching Book of Lists*, by Katherine Perez. Copyright © 2012 by John Wiley & Sons, Inc.

The Co-Teaching Book of Lists

List 5.7   Team-Building Personality Preferences

Looking at Personality Types

One of the most challenging aspects of co-teaching and working with another adult is blending your personalities. It is important to know not only your students' personalities and learning styles, but also the differing personalities in your co-teaching team.

Schools sometimes put two teachers together without taking into consideration their teaching and personality styles. Collaborating together in a co-teaching team requires an understanding of your own personality type and values, along with those of your partner.

If we want relationships to be as productive as they can, we don't want to waste our time misinterpreting each other and misunderstanding the motivation of our partner. Everyone is different, just like our students. It helps when we understand our unique personalities.

What's Important to You?

Review the following characteristics and the associated personality type. Does this describe who you are and what is important to you? Review these characteristics with your co-teaching partner. Determining your personality type will help inform your partnership as you move forward into collaborative planning and teaching together.

Tasks

- Do you need it now?
- Are you focused on deadlines?
- Are you orderly and organized?
- Is it important to finish one thing before starting another task?
- Do you proceed with the end in mind?

Facts

- Concerned with who, what, when, where, why, and how?
- Approach things in a concrete-sequential way?
- Like to make lists?
- Detail oriented?
- Keep track of things?
- Go beneath the surface to find out more?

Collaboration: Working as a Team

People

- Sharing, supportive, a communicator?
- Talkative and like group activities?
- Appreciate discussing issues?
- Are relationships important?
- Prefer working with others instead of independently?

Ideas

- Look at the big picture?
- Conceptualize issues?
- Envision what's more possible?
- Express ideas to others?
- Get to the future early?
- Engage in backwards planning?

List 5.8   Personality Style Activity

What are the strengths of your style? (List four adjectives.)

_____

_____

_____

_____

_____

What are the limitations of your style? (List four adjectives.)

_____

_____

_____

_____

_____

What style would you find the most difficult to work with?

_____

_____

_____

_____

_____

Why would that be challenging for you when co-teaching?

_____

_____

_____

_____

_____

How would co-teaching with someone of a different style be beneficial to your students? Why?

_____

_____

_____

_____

_____

List 5.9 Co-Teaching Conversations

There are many discussions you can have about co-teaching. Review the issues in this section to discuss with your co-teaching partner. Which areas are most important to you? *Prioritize them.* Then schedule a time to begin these conversations, which are critical for team building.

Collaborative Communication

- How do we want to communicate with each other?
  - How frequently should we communicate?
  - What is your preferred method of communication? (in person, by phone, e-mail, text message, or other)
  - Should we take time to communicate outside of school hours?
- What's most important to you?
  - How important is it for you to receive positive reinforcement?
  - What form of feedback is most important to you, and why?
  - What does a good listener do?
  - What "pushes your buttons" in relationships?
- How shall we introduce our partnership?
  - To the students?
  - To parents?
  - How shall we maintain contact with parents?
  - How shall we share our issues with administrators?
- How shall we share constructive feedback with each other?
  - What is the best way to handle disagreements?
  - What procedures should we use to help us with decision making, conflict resolution, and problem solving?
  - How should we negotiate and reach consensus?
- How should we reflect on our co-teaching partnership?
- Areas we need to discuss:
  - Student progress
  - Successes
  - Challenges
  - Next steps
  - How to determine priorities and make adjustments

Classroom Arrangement

- How will we plan and organize the classroom?
  - How will the classroom be arranged? (for traffic patterns and seating arrangements)
  - Should we have a seating chart?
  - How will we make space for flexible groups to meet at the same time?
  - Is there space for both teachers to store materials? For students?
- How will we manage the space in the room?

Curriculum Competence

- How can we ensure that both teachers have the knowledge needed for the specific content and the sequence of instruction?
  - If one teacher is less familiar, how can we develop that knowledge base?
- How can we create an equitable teaching arrangement if one teacher has limited knowledge of accommodations and modifications of curriculum?

Setting Goals and Adjusting Curriculum

- How are we going to collaborate on identifying the essential knowledge and skills to be learned?
- How should we develop the scope and sequence for the upcoming units to be taught? (for example, topics, key ideas, outcomes, activities, projects, and products)
- How will we develop the IEP goals and objectives as a team?
- How will we develop and implement appropriate modifications, adaptations, and accommodations for targeted students?
- How will targeted students be identified? Who will teach them?
- How can we share the responsibility for maintaining and changing the learning centers or stations?

Planning Instruction

- When will we find time to plan?
- How often shall we plan?
- How far ahead should we plan?
- How can we most efficiently and effectively plan as a team?
  - How can we combine the best of our planning processes?
- Do we have a lesson plan format to guide us in our instructional planning that includes:
  - Student learning goals?
  - State standards addressed?
  - Assessment methods?
  - Length of lesson or unit?
  - Sequence of activities or projects?
  - Plans for flexible grouping?
  - Shared teacher roles?
  - Preparation of materials and activities?
  - Ideas for modifications of materials and activities?
- Have we scheduled a regular time to discuss student issues and their progress?

Presenting Content

- What instructional formats and teaching methods do you use most frequently in your classroom (such as lecture, discussion, small-group work, and modeling)
  - Which of these methods are challenging for students with special needs?
  - What are the expected student outcomes? (such as taking notes, pair-shares, outlining key ideas, or graphic organizers)

- ◦ What modifications can be made?
- What techniques do you use to introduce new material?
- What methods do you use for extended learning skills?
- How do you monitor student progress?
- How willing are you to adjust to different ways of teaching?

Assessment and Evaluation

- What forms of informal and authentic assessment should we use?
- How will we balance formative and summative assessment?
- Does homework need to be completed independently, or can it be done collaboratively?
- How will rubrics be developed for student work?
- What criteria will we use to evaluate student work?
  - ◦ How should we grade tests, quizzes, homework, projects, products, and class participation?
  - ◦ Should grades be adjusted for students with special needs?
- How will paperwork be handled on a regular basis?
  - ◦ Grading daily assignments
  - ◦ Reviewing homework
  - ◦ Maintaining records in grade book
  - ◦ Updating IEP data
  - ◦ Taking attendance
  - ◦ Completing report cards or progress reports
  - ◦ Communicating with parents
- How will students be assessed on content? Will choices be offered for students with diverse needs?
- How will assessment be used for ongoing program planning?
- How will we handle participation in and preparation for parent conferences?

Classroom Management

- What classroom management processes will we utilize?
- How should we develop and monitor individual behavior plans?
- What noise levels will we tolerate in the classroom?
- What are the most important procedures and routines to develop?
- What materials are students expected to have or bring to class?

Other Issues

List other key issues you need to discuss that might affect or enhance your teamwork in the co-teaching process.

1. _____
2. _____
3. _____
4. _____

Taken from *The Co-Teaching Book of Lists*, by Katherine Perez. Copyright © 2012 by John Wiley & Sons, Inc.

The Co-Teaching Book of Lists

List 5.10   Co-Teaching Decision Making

Negotiating decisions in a co-taught classroom is an important process and can be a time-consuming issue unless you agree on parameters and procedures in advance.

Decisions that do not require you to consult with your co-teaching partner can be expedited. These decisions include when:

- Time is of the essence
- The issue is low priority
- The outcome has little significance
- The decision is best made by one person
- Decisions are predetermined
- The outcome is not critical to the success of the program

However, there are times when team decision making is important to your program. Team decision making is best when:

- The decision or outcome may have a direct impact on your program
- The broader the input, the more valuable the input
- The issue is multifaceted
- The implications of the decision will directly affect your program
- Multiple perspectives are needed

Solution-Based Focus

The following questions will help you as a team to guide decision making:

- What is the easiest and quickest solution?
- Which idea aligns best with our goals for our students?
- Can this idea be supported by the necessary resources?
- What is the most enduring solution that will last the longest?
- Which solution would be the least intrusive to our program?
- Which solution best fits the goals for our co-teaching program?
- What idea fits best with the research on effective instruction?
- Which solution would enhance our program?
- What idea would provide the least interruption to our program?

List 5.11   Potential Challenges

What are some of the challenges, problems, or obstacles that might interfere with a cohesive collaborative relationship with your co-teacher? Let's examine some of these more closely now and the impact that each one may have on the success of your program.

Teaching Methods and Beliefs

- Examining your perspective on education and your values and beliefs is especially important
- Some obstacles emerge as a result of differing viewpoints of the co-teachers regarding instructional techniques
- Different approaches to classroom management policies and procedures in particular can cause conflict

Personality Style and Differences

- Personality differences may cause discord in a partnership if one teacher is more relaxed on procedures and routines and the other teacher is much more strict about adherence to rules in the classroom
- When two teachers have very different approaches to teaching, it is difficult to find a balance
- Clear communication is always the best solution
- When co-teaching, the classroom is under the equal guidance of both teachers
- Decide on mutually acceptable norms of behavior, and establish procedures and routines together

Compliance Issues

- Meeting the needs of students with special needs involves fulfilling the legal requirements of their IEP; however, this can become a roadblock if the special education teacher handles all compliance issues and appropriate modifications in the curriculum
- Co-teaching needs to be a shared responsibility
- The general education teacher is ultimately responsible for the education of all students in the classroom; this is especially true with the current mandates of No Child Left Behind

Misperceptions of What Should Be

- Two teachers often enter the co-teaching situation with specific ideas about how things should be and how things should be accomplished
- Differing opinions can cause friction if they are not discussed ahead of time
- Clear communication is the key to success in overcoming this hurdle

Content Area Knowledge

- The credibility of the co-teachers could be questioned if the special education teacher lacks sufficient knowledge of the content or subject matter of the class

- The credibility of the general education teacher might likewise be questioned if the teacher lacks specific techniques for curriculum modifications and adaptations for students with special needs
- Both teachers need to take the time to share their expectations with each other
- Both teachers need to share their specific fields of expertise with each other

Lack of Time

- Collaboration takes time
- In addition to weekly planning meetings, you need to allow time to make the modifications required in the curriculum for students with special needs
- You should also allow time to ponder the possibilities of differentiating the content, process, and products of the lessons
- Consideration must be given to the time it takes for the teachers to develop this important process
- Often teachers are overscheduled, have added paperwork, or are asked to perform crisis intervention for their colleagues at a moment's notice

Lack of External Support

- Site administrators are the key to co-teaching success
- They typically design the master schedule, which affects the placement of students in co-taught classrooms
- Administrators are also responsible for ensuring proper preparation time and co-planning time for the teachers
- Professional development on issues of inclusion usually needs administrative endorsement
- Without these supports in place and adequate resources supplied, there may be obstacles to the successful implementation of co-teaching at the site
- Sometimes the administrator has no control of the implementation and may simply state: "This is a legal requirement; we need to do it, and you are responsible"

List 5.12   Overcoming Roadblocks: Solutions

Here are some tips to overcome some of those potential roadblocks you might encounter in a co-taught classroom:

Be Flexible

- Flexibility is key and a vital trait for co-teachers
- If teachers are rigid, the program will falter and its effectiveness will be diminished
- Your relationship will be stronger and your students will be better served with flexibility and an open mind as to the possibilities

Focus on Both Co-Teachers' Strengths

- Your combined strengths will help you solve the challenges you face
- Learn to celebrate your expertise and talents
- Sharing your assets and experiences with your students will benefit the entire program

All Students Are Shared by Both Co-Teachers

- The purpose of co-teaching is collaboration
- The program also reduces the stigma of special education labels
- Both teachers need to work with all the students in the class, regardless of which co-teaching approach used

List 5.13   Dealing with Conflict

There are triggers in the classroom that can easily set off our frustration. Handling conflict in a constructive way takes practice and pausing to think before you act. When you are faced with conflict, take a moment to pause and reflect on your reactions carefully.

Stop and Think

- Change your negative thoughts to positive possibilities
- Consider personality type and teaching style
- Visualize yourself being successful in this interaction
- Reframe the situation—what are other perspectives?
- Seek support and alternative suggestions from colleagues
- Affirm to yourself how you will handle this situation
- Get rid of any negative self-talk and any put-downs from your partner; these will only lead to anger and dissatisfaction
- Tell yourself that you can handle this, and assume that your partner is trying their best and is not out to annoy you
- Take a step back and carefully reflect on the situation
- Plan a possible solution

Get away from statements that will stagnate any sort of resolution:

- It won't work!
- It's too hard.
- I can't do that.
- Where will we get the money for that?
- That idea is ridiculous!
- *No!*
- That's against policy.
- Out of the question.
- You've got to be kidding!
- It takes too much time.
- I'm not interested.
- No way

Instead, try a more positive perspective:

- Use I-statements to express your own thoughts, and consider paraphrasing your co-teacher's ideas
- Visualize your interaction and your success in this interaction
- Frame your actions, thoughts, and words in positive ways
- Some people find it helpful to pause and say nothing; others find it easier to speak up and share their perspective openly

- Sometimes you can avoid conflict at the onset by acknowledging the other person's statement and moving on, instead of getting involved with the issues and going on the defensive

Here are some positive statements that tend to diffuse conflict:

- "Thank you for letting me know how you feel"
- "I will give that idea some thought"
- "I am sorry that you were upset; that was not my intent"
- "I will talk to you soon when I am calm"
- "I understand"
- "I hear you; perhaps you are right"
- "I see that this upsets you"
- "Excuse me, but I have more to say"
- "That is an interesting perspective on this issue"

Knowing the right words to say to stop conflict is only one piece of the conflict-avoidance puzzle. We send messages not only through our words, but also through our body language and tone of voice:

- A calm voice and a neutral body stance can help diffuse a negative reaction
- Be conscious of your body language and the words you choose when exchanging ideas with your co-teacher

Successful Collaboration Strategies

- Discuss issues with your co-teaching partner only
- Always look for successes—what worked well with your co-teacher?
- Compliment your colleague whenever you can
- Remain flexible
- Be thoughtful—unexpected appreciation cards mean a lot

The Co-Teaching Book of Lists

List 5.14 Steps to Take

Define the Problem or Issue

- See it as an opportunity for growth
- Use active listening and I-statements
- Be clear and agree that it is a problem and what the problem is
- Look at implications for the future of your program
- Focus on your primary need or desired outcome
- If you have difficulty reaching a resolution, ask yourself why

Generate Solutions by Brainstorming

- Look at possibilities as rapidly as possible without judgment, and write them all down
- See differences as possible positive solutions
- Expand, extend, and combine the ideas of others
- Record all ideas; don't explain

Evaluate Possible Solutions to Try

- Each teacher suggests some possible solutions
- Each possibility is discussed
- How do solutions address needs?
- Are the solutions feasible? Easily implemented?
- Discuss advantages and challenges for each option
- Narrow down solutions that meet your needs
- If you are unable to decide, elicit advice from other colleagues
- Choose the best possible solution, considering all factors

Plan the Implementation Process

- Decide who, what, where, why, when, and how
- Develop an action plan to implement the solution
- Agree on how the possible solution will be implemented and who will do what
- Put your plan in writing
- Reach agreement on implementation

Evaluate the Plan and Outcomes

- Develop a method to evaluate plan
- Decide when you will evaluate the plan
- Set a date to check on how the plan is going
- Decide how you will evaluate the success of the plan
- What outcomes were achieved?
- What worked best about this solution?
- How can we improve on the plan in the future?
- Make changes as needed

Collaboration: Working as a Team

List 5.15   Communication and Accountability Tools

Clear, consistent communication and organization are essential ingredients in a co-teaching relationship between the general educator, special educator, paraprofessional, specialist and administrator:

- Frequent and ongoing communication is important; setting a structure and specified time to talk is vital to ongoing success
- Systems should be established to discuss issues, organize instruction, and handle concerns of the classroom to facilitate collaboration

Evaluating the Co-Teaching Process

Following are some issues to consider when you are evaluating the co-teaching process. This conversation should be scheduled at regular intervals and should be ongoing.

- Evaluation is not just an opportunity for discussion; the results of the evaluation should be shared with your administrator
- Making your administrator aware of important issues, especially the positive gains, should result in greater overall support of the program; if you present concerns to the administrator, be sure you also offer possible solutions

List 5.16   Checking In: How Is Our Co-Teaching Going?

- Are you differentiating instruction to meet the diverse needs of your students?
- Is your focus on the middle with grade-level learners? Advanced learners? Lower-achieving students?
- Do the students feel that both teachers are there to help them?
- Do the students know which are the students with special needs? How are they treated in class?
- How will you determine students' perceptions of your class?
- How are general education students doing in the co-taught classroom? Are they reaching higher standards?
- Have you noticed social and behavioral benefits in your co-taught classroom?
- How is this program benefiting students with IEPs?
- Are you using centers and flexible grouping to adapt to the specific needs of your students?
- Is the shared workload equitable and consistent?
- Do you feel your expertise is being utilized to maximize the success of all the students in your classroom?
- What would you like to see improved?
- What is going well in your program?
- What changes should you make?
- Do you have a regularly scheduled time to meet and plan?
- Is your planning time being used effectively?

Communication Cards

Since frequent and ongoing communication is essential to a co-teaching program, why not try a quick communication card strategy? Using three-by-five-inch index cards, your prompts could include:

- What's working?
- What's not working?
- An idea to try . . .

This quick exchange can be delivered in person or placed in your co-teacher's mailbox for future reflection. It is important to keep these ideas flowing and to be proactive in sharing your feelings and ideas.

List 5.17   Collaborative Problem-Solving Worksheet

Issue to Be Discussed _____

Date _____

Desired Outcomes:

Possible Solutions	Advantages/Disadvantages
○ _____	○ _____
○ _____	○ _____
○ _____	○ _____
○ _____	○ _____
○ _____	○ _____
○ _____	○ _____

Solution to be tried first

ACTION PLAN

Implementation Steps	Who?	By When?	Where?
_____	_____	_____	_____
_____	_____	_____	_____
_____	_____	_____	_____
_____	_____	_____	_____

How and when will progress be evaluated?

What worked best with this problem solving, and how can we improve it?

Chapter 6

Organizing and Planning for Success

List 6.1   Celebrating *All* Learners: Strategies for Success

---

Building a Caring Classroom Community

Make your co-teaching classroom a *Cheers!* classroom, the kind "where everybody knows your name." One of the main purposes of the co-teaching process is to create an inclusive environment that is free from labels and the stigma of "being different." To do that, we need to create a caring community that honors diversity.

There are several factors to consider in organizing your classroom for co-teaching:

- Physical organization of the room
- Classroom procedures and routines
- Classroom climate
- Classroom management
- Classroom expectation
- Classroom agreements: the conditions we need to work together

---

By changing your classroom environment to become more inclusive, you can deliver more content in a more meaningful way. In this chapter we will look at the various facets of classroom organization. In order to ensure greater engagement, we will look at various flexible grouping patterns to support learning.

- Everything in your classroom sends important messages to the learner—are these messages positive or negative?
- Your classroom organization affects students' ability to focus on and retain information and support learning outcomes
- The social outcomes of co-teaching programs are almost as important as the academic outcomes

Here are some tips for enhancing inclusion in your classroom:

- Instill a can-do spirit in the class
- Promote the belief that *all* students can succeed
- Make sure students know that all learners are welcome here
- Keep high expectations for everyone—do not "water down" the curriculum
- Learn more about your students:
  - Academic history
  - Learning styles
  - Interest surveys
  - Personal profiles of strengths
  - Multiple intelligences
  - Parent surveys

The Co-Teaching Book of Lists

- Focus with your co-teaching partner on differentiated activities that support all students
- Celebrate their strengths and use these strengths to help students grow and learn
- Make sure your classroom is a safe environment for everyone to learn
- Risk taking and mistakes should be encouraged and seen as learning opportunities
- Involve choice in the selection of activities, projects, and products
- Empower the students to collaborate with you and the co-teacher to establish classroom procedures, routines, and expectations
- Using positive language, have students work with you to develop the conditions needed to work together in your caring classroom
- Be patient with yourself, your co-teacher, and your students—remember that this is a new process for all of you
- Use activators to engage students at the beginning of a lesson and summarizers to check for understanding at the end of a lesson
- Try to integrate a classroom meeting into each day or week where students can share what is on their minds, celebrate their successes, and solve problems or concerns together
- Start a Student of the Week bulletin board, where only positive pitches are allowed to be shared in celebrating the student
- Decide on the positive reinforcement methods you will use
- Always consider your classroom a learning community where you are helping one another grow
- Assure students that they will be successful in the classroom if they put forth their best effort to learn
- Create "walls of wonder" in your classroom space that reinforce your positive, caring community
- Have students create slogans around the theme of a caring classroom, put them on sentence strips, and post them around the room
- Share stories, poems, and articles about acceptance and tolerance
- Teach specific conflict resolution techniques and model these steps for students
- Promote sharing of differing cultural and linguistic backgrounds and set aside time to celebrate the various cultures in the classroom
- Explore online resources (such as those in List 6.2) that celebrate the unique differences of all your learners and strategies for teaching

List 6.2   Helpful Online Resources

www.operationrespect.org Free downloads of curriculum, music, and activities to promote respectful, caring classrooms; also includes anti-bullying lessons and resources

www.actsofkindness.org   Ideas and strategies for promoting kindness in your classroom

www.teachtolerance.org   resources, articles, literature, and lessons on the acceptance of others

www.responsiveclassroom.org   Ideas about morning meetings and class-building activities

www.kaganonline.com   Ideas on cooperative learning, student engagement, and varied grouping structures

www.inclusiveschools.org   Ideas for children's literature selections celebrating student differences

www.rubistar.com   Great ideas for designing rubrics

www.educationoasis.com   Resources for graphic organizers

www.powerof2.org   Strategies, learning modules, and teaching materials for co-teaching classrooms

www.ldonline.org   Information, teaching strategies, and assessment tools

www.cec.sped.org   Curriculum ideas for various students with special needs, resources, journal articles, and discussion forums

www.ku.crl.org   Resources for the Strategic Instruction Model from the University of Kansas Center for Research on Learning

www.parrotpublishing.com   Online book on collaboration; teaching resources

www.inspiration.com and www.kidspiration.com   Helpful tools for students to organize information

www.mastrmnds@aol.com and www.graphicorganizers.com   Resources and templates for graphic organizers

www.texthelp.com   Text-to-speech software with free downloads

www.brighteye.com   A hand-held scanner used to read and translate text

www.humanware.com   Text-to-speech conversion with adjustable rates and different language options

www.rfbd.org   Reading for blind and dyslexic students, books on tape, and resources

www.newhorizons.org   Database of inclusion resources, strategies, and research by the Washington State Department of Education

www.help4teachers.com   Resources for tiered lessons, various subjects, and grade levels

www.parentsplace.com   Parent resource center, materials, and information to share

www.edc.org/FSC/NCIP   National Center to Improve Practice in Special Education

www.inclusion.com   Inclusion resources

List 6.3   Physical Organization

The physical setting of the co-taught classroom has a definite impact on the success of co-teaching and promoting positive acceptance of all learners. Here are some techniques for more effective use of space in your classroom:

- The lighting, seating arrangement, room temperature, and sounds in the classroom environment should be modified to adjust to the needs of the students and the content of the lesson
- Carefully consider how you can facilitate student mobility in the classroom by the arrangement of the furniture; the room should be arranged for maximum movement by teachers and students
- Areas in the room should have clear physical boundaries that are conducive to learning (such as a large-group instruction area and a small-group area)
- Make sure students are physically comfortable with the setup and furnishings in the classroom
- The learning environment should be organized to minimize visual and auditory distractions for greater student focus
- Make sure that materials and resources are well organized and clearly labeled to promote student independence and to facilitate task management
- The physical space of the classroom should allow for varied groupings depending on learning goals
- Allow for varied levels of energy and noise in the classroom depending on the goal or task—from relaxed, focused learning to rigorous investigations
- Establish and post routines and procedures in the classroom so that everyone understands the expectations for collecting assignments, working in groups, sharpening pencils, raising hands, obtaining resources, and so on
- Support rules and procedures with visual representations
- Provide adequate physical space for both teachers
- Ensure that the room reinforces the message of a positive environment to support all students succeed
- Lesson-plan book should be readily accessible for both teachers to use
- Make sure it is apparent that *both* teachers are equal partners in the classroom: both names should be on the outside door and on the board
- Each student should have a storage space within his or her reach, and it should be clearly labeled
- Work assignments should be in containers that are clearly labeled
- Materials and educational resources areas should be clearly marked so that students can find them easily and replace them in their appropriate space
- For younger students, specific areas should be designated for group activities, centers, break time, and workstations
- The schedule should be posted, explained, and practiced for greater understanding
- Activity charts, agendas, routines, and stations should include visual supports so that they are easily understood
- Keep a list of rotating "experts" in the classroom so that students know they can get help from someone other than the teachers at all times

List 6.4   Strategies for Flexible Grouping

Students in a co-teaching classroom have diverse learning styles and needs and have their own unique entry points to learning. Therefore, flexible grouping is vital for creating a supportive environment that is responsive to their individual needs and for more effectively delivering the instruction.

Teaching to meet those individual needs requires flexibility in grouping patterns to avoid "sit-and-get" lectures that do not facilitate retention.

Planning for Grouping: Similar Readiness

- Preassess for readiness levels
- Use student work samples to determine placement
- Use formative assessment to adjust groupings
- "Kid-watch" for readiness
- Make sure these groups are fluid, not fixed

Interests

- Groups will change according to student interest inventories
- Class discussions
- Personal profiles

How Students Learn Best

- According to learning style
- Multiple intelligences
- Alone, in pairs, or in groups
- In accordance with classroom observation

Student Choice

- Within a range of options
- Students select
- Selected by random draw

List 6.5   Small-Group Strategies

Questions to Consider

When you are beginning to form small groups, ask yourself the following questions:

- How will we decide on the learning targets and goals for the groups?
- What data will we base our grouping decisions on?
- How often will data be collected and evaluated?
- How will we decide on the size of the groups?
- How will students be assigned to small groups (by student choice, teacher choice, or at random)?
- Who will teach each group?
- What will the group lesson look like?
- What activities and materials will be needed?
- How much movement of students might be expected in the groups?
- Will some students work in an independent group?
- How will that be determined?
- Who will monitor the task completion of the independent group?
- Who will design materials for the group and assess the effectiveness of the lesson?
- How will we differentiate activities for our groups?
- How will you support students who need assistance?
- How will the two teachers communicate about the outcomes of the groups and the progress that the students made?
- What activators and summarizers have you planned for the groups?
- How will you check for understanding?

Promoting Successful Small-Group Learning

- Carefully explain the task to the students
- Explain the criteria and standards for success
- Specify the learning objectives and expected outcomes for the group
- Arrange the physical environment in the room to facilitate small-group structures
- Determine which materials and resources will be needed for each group and how these will be distributed
- Decide on appropriate group roles depending on task and how these roles will be determined (by teacher, student, or random draw)
- Specify the desired behaviors and expectations of each group
- Decide on time allocation for small-group work and post this information for all to see
- Discuss expectations for group and individual accountability
- Set up a system to monitor student behavior
- Intervene if necessary to teach collaboration skills and conflict resolution issues
- Evaluate the quality of student work accomplished
- Discuss with the students their assessment of how the group functioned and what was accomplished

List 6.6   Working Together for Small-Group Success

Keep these strategies in mind as you discuss with your co-teacher about implementing small-group instruction. You both need to be involved in the planning, delivery, and implementation of groups in order for them to be successful.

- Start small-group work gradually, especially if you and your co-teacher are just beginning the process
- Share your expectations with the students and engage them in a discussion of the desired outcomes and accountability
- Do a Y-chart activity as a large group: discuss what a successful small group looks like, feels like, and sounds like, then discuss ideas (see Chapter Nine for more information)
- Agree on behavioral norms for group work
- Let the students know that their group is accountable for work accomplished collectively as well as individually; decide how this will be measured
- Discuss your feedback on the outcomes of groups often so students clearly understand what is acceptable and what is expected of them
- Have students complete a brief feedback sheet to find out what worked well and what the next steps should be
- Make sure one co-teacher is available during small-group time for additional support; one teacher can directly facilitate a small group while the other one roams and observes other groups and responds to questions
- Observe positive group interactions and note these during group discussion time
- You can move gradually to a model where both teachers are facilitating different small groups as procedures are refined and implemented; there can also be an independent group where the teacher checks on progress only occasionally
- Be flexible about the time allowed for each small group activity; some groups may need extended time or support depending on the nature of the task to be accomplished
- Have anchor activities readily available if a group finishes early, so that everyone is still engaged in learning
- Carefully decide which tasks are most suitable for small-group work, and be realistic; if the task is too complex, more time or teacher support may be needed
- If students are new to small-group work, start out gradually and have them work with a learning partner successfully first, before moving them to a larger group of four to six students
- If you and your co-teacher are actively involved in small-group instruction at the same time, establish procedures for students to obtain help and support as needed; for example, designate three students as "expert helpers" of the week and have students go to one of them first for assistance

- Collaborative small groups can become quite noisy, so decide ahead of time on the appropriate noise level for the task and discuss noise level tolerance with students; sometimes it helps to play soft classical music in the background while they work
- Transitions and movement need to be modeled and described before the grouping begins; the key is to minimize movement for maximum efficiency and effectiveness
- Assign various roles to the students to assist you and your co-teacher during the small-group process: some students can be "resource managers" for the group, while others can be designated as "questioners" who ask questions when clarification is needed; another student can be the "reporter" who shares the main ideas to the larger group, and another the "recorder" to record main ideas for whole-class discussion

Organizing and Planning for Success

List 6.7   Advantages of Small-Group Instruction

In order to maximize the benefits of small-group work in a co-taught classroom, teachers need to take time to plan the lessons carefully, keeping in mind the techniques previously described.

Taking Time to Plan

- Lessons should be planned collaboratively
- Insights about student needs, possible grouping, and instructional content should be discussed together
- Use a variety of grouping strategies to improve use of teacher time
- Plan how students can be more involved in the teaching-and-learning process, learning not only from their teachers, but also from each other and on their own

Meeting Diverse Needs

Utilizing small, flexible groups in your co-teaching classroom allows you to meet the unique and diverse needs of all of your learners. The advantages in your classroom are many:

- Small groups enable teachers to focus instruction on specific needs and targeted goals at various readiness levels
- Small groups provide students greater access to both teachers and reduce the student-teacher ratio for specific lessons
- Lessons can be adjusted for necessary scaffolding or accelerated for advanced learners to extend and enrich the curriculum
- Small groups can be formed according to the learning styles of the students to increase their access to the curriculum and maximize success
- Teachers can be more responsive to individual needs with on-the-spot interventions and modifications
- Pacing of lessons can be adjusted depending on the needs of the group
- Teachers can differentiate the assessment of the outcomes of the lesson for specific groups

Coordination and Communication

- Teachers will be more informed about the individual progress of their students as a result of small-group instruction
- Instruction can be adjusted depending on the needs of the small groups
- Teachers need to coordinate the sharing of results from the groups to inform their future planning

The Co-Teaching Book of Lists

List 6.8   Small-Group Planning

Class _____

Teachers _____

Date _____

What will students know, understand, or be able to do as a result of instruction?	What co-teaching model will we use? How will students be grouped?	What instruction will be differentiated? What data will be used to guide our decisions?
Group #1 Group #2 Independent Group		
Teacher #1 responsibilities:	Teacher #2 responsibilities:	How or when will we process and debrief?

List 6.9   Points to Ponder: Large-Group Instruction

Direct teaching takes place with large-group instruction. This is a necessary part of any co-taught classroom. It is essential that students hear the same message before teachers plan to differentiate the content, process, and product of the lesson. Here are some points to ponder to maximize the success of large-group instruction:

- Discuss the advantages of large-group instruction for this lesson: Is there another approach that might be more effective?
- How will both teachers actively participate during large-group instruction?
- What are the specific outcomes of the lesson to be taught?
- What should students know, understand, and be able to do as a result of the lesson?
- What co-teaching approach maximizes the effect of the content to be covered?
- Is it possible to divide the class and do parallel teaching regarding the same content?
- How will you check for understanding before deciding on the next step?
- What formative assessment process will you use to inform your decision?

List 6.10   Planning for Large-Group Instruction

Class _____

Teachers _____

Date _____

What will students know, understand, or be able to do as a result of instruction?	What co-teaching model will we use?	What materials will be needed? What technology will be utilized?
Teacher #1 responsibilities:	Teacher #2 responsibilities:	How or when will we process and debrief?

List 6.11 Independent Student Work

In a co-taught classroom, positive and productive independent classroom behaviors are essential to maximize time on task and application of content. However, students need to be instructed about the work habits needed for independent work.

Procedures

Some of the important procedures for teaching and modeling appropriate independent work include:

- Where do students obtain necessary materials?
- How do they use the resources for the assignment?
- What are the outcomes and parameters of the work to be completed?
- What does successful completion look like?
- How will students be assessed on their performance?
- How will they seek help if needed?
- How much time do they have for completion?

With this basic foundation implemented, the co-teachers will be more readily available to work with individual students or small-group intervention work.

Expectations

- Lessons are well explained and outcomes described
- Possible independent learning contracts are drafted
- Students know where to keep their ongoing independent work and materials
- Students know when assignments are due and where to turn them in
- Students are provided with various record-keeping forms for data collection purposes
- Provide students with a carefully designed sequence of tasks to be completed; after demonstrating mastery of independent work, students might be able to prioritize the scope of work completion on their own
- Provide students with anchor activities to pursue when work is completed early; this work should be kept in a specified part of the classroom and should provide needed enrichment and/or extension activities related to content

Managing Materials

Procedures also need to be in place so that students know the acceptable procedures for dealing with classroom materials:

- How to obtain materials and equipment needed for task completion
- Techniques for transporting materials and supplies to designated work areas so as not to disrupt the rest of the class
- Students should use classroom supplies as directed
- Students should notify teachers when supplies are low
- Students should not waste materials

The Co-Teaching Book of Lists

Success Strategies

- When assigning independent work, make sure it is at the appropriate level for that particular student
- Assignments should be familiar to the students and used as an extension or enrichment of a direct teaching lesson already provided
    - Make sure you model the concepts to be learned to students before independent work commences
    - Provide necessary guided practice with support so that you can observe student understanding
    - Provide frequent and ongoing observation and feedback to students during the independent work phase for adequate support

Seeking Support

Students engaged in independent work should know how to:

- Let the teacher(s) know when they need help, without disrupting a small-group lesson; students can post a small "Stop" sign on desk as a silent signal and do an anchor activity until teacher is free to give guidance
- Discuss questions with peers who may know the answer
- Move on to another activity in the lesson until the teacher is available to help
- Sign up on a Help Wanted sheet on the bulletin board to notify teachers of their need

List 6.12   Goal Setting: Keeping Score

Student name _____

Date _____

My Goal(s):			
Day of the Week	Number of Times My Goal Was Met (Use Tally)	My Signature or Initials	Teacher Signature or Initials
Monday			
Tuesday			
Wednesday			
Thursday			
Friday			

Student Self-Survey

Name _____

Date _____

1. Did I set a learning goal for myself?	Yes	No
2. Did I accomplish my goal?	Yes	No
3. Did I work cooperatively with others?	Yes	No
4. Did I assist others who needed help?	Yes	No
5. Did I take turns?	Yes	No
6. Did I participate actively in class?	Yes	No
7. Did I listen to directions?	Yes	No
8. Did I ask for help when I needed it?	Yes	No
9. Did I follow directions?	Yes	No
10. Did I complete class assignments in a timely way?	Yes	No
11. Did I turn in completed assignments?	Yes	No
12. Do I understand the homework assignments?	Yes	No

List 6.13   Choices, Not Chance, in Your Curriculum

Once students have been successful with independent work and have clearly demonstrated self-motivation to complete tasks, teachers may decide to build in some choices. It is important that these choices be carefully developed and not left to chance. Therefore, students need to know:

- Where they can work without disturbing the other learning activities that are occurring concurrently
- How to navigate the room with the least amount of disruption when obtaining materials and returning them
- How to sustain a productive work time and extend it as needed
- When to change tasks and move on to other assignments
- The limits, capacity, and other parameters of the various learning centers
- Whether talking with others is permitted—what procedures are in place?
- How to record progress and completion of certain tasks

List 6.14   Procedures and Routines

Collaborating on appropriate procedures and routines is an important process for co-teachers to engage in before the students arrive, so that the classroom can be both efficient and effective.

- Procedures should reflect the way you do things to be successful
- Routines require repeated practice and modeling
- All students should be educated in a safe and secure learning environment
- If you make classroom procedures predictable, it will take the guesswork out of navigating your classroom
- Routines that are carefully orchestrated promote self-confidence and independence in learners
- Students take pride in their accomplishments and work more cooperatively toward the learning targets
- Self-esteem is enhanced when students clearly know expectations up front

List 6.15   Co-Teaching Conversations

During your initial co-planning time, you may want to discuss the following issues to ensure a cohesive and organized classroom environment.

In What Ways Can We . . .

- Organize our time to work with individuals, small groups, and the whole group?
- Provide opportunities for students to learn in the ways they learn best?
- Develop classroom materials and modifications to better meet the individual needs of the learners?
- Pay attention to the pacing of the curriculum and make adjustments as necessary?
- Make homework more student-centered, purposeful, and useful to the students?
- Increase student responsibility for the completion and quality of their work?
- Match classroom tasks to individual student needs?
- Develop authentic assessments that align with the curriculum, measure what a student knows and is able to do, and are ongoing and formative?

List 6.16   Routines That Are Important for Co-Teachers to Share

- Expectations for the start of class, such as bell work and warm-ups
- Expectations for students when unpacking items
- How students obtain and put away materials
- Where students should put notes from home
- How to maximize the use of time wisely
- How students will keep and submit records of their work for feedback
- Acceptable transition techniques between activities, lessons, or groups
- Understanding scheduling issues: where they should be and when
- Where to post the schedule so that everyone understands the duration and flow of activities
- What to do when students need help and the teacher is not available
- Ideas and expectations for the end of class each day, including reflection and summarizer activities
- Who to notify when students are absent for the day

The Co-Teaching Book of Lists

List 6.17   Looking at Your Classroom from a Student's Perspective

- Where do I put my backpack, books, jacket, and other stuff?
- Where do I find my assignments?
- Where are the materials I need to do my assignments?
- What do I do when I arrive at class?
- Where do I go? Is there a seating chart?
- How do I get the teacher's attention when I need help?
- What do I do when my work is done?

Meeting Student Needs

- Students need a clear understanding of behavioral and curriculum expectations
- Curriculum needs to be "chunked," carefully sequenced, and scaffolded for student success
- The classroom environment should be relaxed, predictable, and calm
- Be sure to start each activity with an activator and end with a summarizer so that beginnings and endings of lessons are clear to students
- Content of lessons should be meaningful and engaging
- Information should be presented both verbally and visually for greater comprehension by students with different learning styles
- Materials should be presented in ways that help students focus on essential information
- Promote independence and self-confidence on the part of the learners by incorporating choice in the curriculum
- Clarify how students need to transition from one activity to the next
- Provide opportunities to generalize information and provide feedback to students

List 6.18   Additional Procedure Pointers

Demonstrate and use hand signals or sign language for students to:

- Speak more quietly
- Turn in work
- Prepare for transition time
- Switch tasks or groups
- Prepare for end of class
- Return to task and improve behavior

Use three-by-five-inch goal or task cards for students to indicate:

- Steps to complete an assignment
- Estimated time to complete
- Reminders of goals
- Checkpoint for feedback from teacher

Model or demonstrate what each of these procedures for smooth transitions look like:

- Students leaving for another class
- Transitioning from one group to another
- Gathering materials
- Putting away materials
- Lining up for lunch
- Leaving for home

The Co-Teaching Book of Lists

List 6.19   Supporting Student Behavior

Conditions Needed to Work Together

Develop a list of conditions needed to work together in your classroom collaboratively with the students. What is important for them as members of this classroom community? Some examples might include:

- We will respect each other's needs
- We will come to class on time and be prepared to learn
- We will listen attentively to each other and to the teacher
- We will take turns talking and allow for everyone to participate in the discussion
- We will be fully present in class and not distracted by other things
- We will interact with each other with respect and positive intentions, not with put-downs

These norms should be agreed upon by the entire class and posted in a prominent position for all to see. When someone experiences an infraction of these conditions, they can point it out on the chart to steer the behavior back to a positive track.

List 6.20   Classroom Rules That Work

In collaboration with the students, create a list of classroom rules, keeping the "conditions we need to work together" in mind.

- Students need clear behavioral expectations in a co-teaching situation as well as consequences
- Some students may need an individualized behavior intervention contract to help them better understand classroom rules
- Both co-teachers need to agree on the expected appropriate behaviors and the consequences for infractions
- Be consistent in enforcing your classroom management system in the classroom

Some pointers to help you in this process include:

- Frame classroom rules in a positive manner; they should be more than a list of "don'ts"
- Have students participate in generating the classroom rules
- "Catch the students being good" and reinforce those positive behaviors
- Keep the rules simple and basic; try to set no more than four to six key conditions
- Model the rules for the students so they clearly understand expectations
- Have the students practice and role-play what the rules look like in practice
- Determine an effective and positive reinforcement system and be consistent
- Plan activities that are within the range of the students' ability, to keep frustration and acting-out behaviors at a minimum
- Calmly, quietly, and quickly approach and redirect students who are off task using a nonverbal cue or a cue card that is unobtrusive
- Use proximity control (the co-teaching classroom makes this much more feasible)
- Discuss logical consequences with the students, stressing fairness
- Consequences should be reasonable and relevant
- Decide on a conflict resolution plan
- Show the students how they can self-monitor the implementation of these rules in the classroom
- Inform the parents of the rules so that they can be partners in the process
- The most important factor in managing behavior is responding to the problem behavior consistently

The Co-Teaching Book of Lists

List 6.21   Behavior Intervention Worksheet

This worksheet can be used by the co-teaching team with specific, targeted students who need intervention for behavioral concerns. It is for *planning purposes only* and may serve as a useful tool for monitoring the progress of certain students and keeping track of interventions used. You may wish to include the student in the team meeting, if it seems appropriate.

Student _____

Grade _____

Class or Period _____

Date _____

Co-Teachers _____

Describe inappropriate behavior observed:

_____

_____

_____

_____

Describe the situation that preceded behavior:

_____

_____

_____

_____

Specify the target behavior(s) to be modified:

_____

_____

_____

_____

Describe any intervention approaches previously used:

_____

_____

_____

_____

Brainstorm a list of potential approaches to try:

_____

_____

_____

_____

Describe new behavior goals (include consequences and reinforcers):

_____

_____

_____

_____

Signed _____

Date of review _____

Source: Adapted from K. Kryza, *Practical Inclusion Strategies: Maximizing Student Success in the Inclusive Classroom (Grades 6–12)* (Bellevue, WA: Bureau of Education and Research, 2007).

The Co-Teaching Book of Lists

List 6.22   Student Survey

Student _____

Date _____

1. What is your favorite subject at school?
   ◦ Reading
   ◦ Writing
   ◦ Math
   ◦ Science
   ◦ Spelling
   ◦ History
   ◦ Other _____
2. What do you enjoy most about school? Why?
3. What do enjoy least about school? Why?
4. Do you prefer to work:
   ◦ Alone?
   ◦ In groups?
   ◦ With a partner?
   ◦ Why?
5. What hobbies and activities do you have outside of school? (such as clubs, sports, or crafts)
6. How much time do you spend watching TV each day?

   _____

7. What are your favorite TV shows?

   _____

8. How much time do you spend on the computer each day?

   _____

9. What do you like to do on the computer?
10. What types of music do you listen to?

    _____

    _____

11. How do you learn best in school?

    _____

12. What is the most important thing in your life?

    _____

13. What are your goals for the future?

    _____

14. What should your teacher know about you that will help you do your best in school?

    _____

Source: Adapted from K. Kryza, *Practical Inclusion Strategies: Maximizing Student Success in the Inclusive Classroom (Grades 6–12)* (Bellevue, WA: Bureau of Education and Research, 2007). Used with permission.

List 6.23   How Are You Smart? Multiple Intelligences Survey

Directions. Below you will find listed the eight types of intelligence. Listed under each type of intelligence are some descriptions of activities that relate to that type of intelligence. Read the descriptions and check the boxes that describe you. Go with your first instinct. Then total the number you checked at the bottom of each intelligence section. At the end, transfer each total to the intelligence graph and see what your strongest intelligences are. Remember—most people are strong in more than one type of intelligence. Have fun!

Intelligence #1

_____ I can hear or see words in my head before I speak or write them.

_____ I like games such as Scrabble, Jeopardy, Trivial Pursuit, word searches, and crosswords.

_____ I enjoy writing and have received praise and/or recognition for my writing talents.

_____ I often talk about things that I have read or heard.

_____ I love to read books, magazines, anything!

_____ I am good with words. I learn and use new words in creative and/or funny ways regularly.

_____ When I am in a classroom, I pay attention to all the written posters and the writing on the board.

_____ I have a very good memory for hearing and seeing words.

TOTAL _____

Intelligence #2

_____ I enjoy activities like dancing, swimming, biking, or skating.

_____ I play a sport or do physical activity regularly.

_____ I need to do things with my hands or by moving in order to learn them best.

_____ I am good at imitating others and like drama and acting.

_____ I use my hands and body when I am talking with someone.

_____ I need to move around a lot and change positions often when sitting.

_____ I need to touch things to learn about them.

TOTAL _____

Intelligence #3

_____ I like to draw and doodle.

_____ I am good at finding my way around places I don't know well.

_____ I can easily see in my head how furniture would fit in a room. I am good at jigsaw puzzles.

_____ I remember things better if I can draw or create an image of them.

_____ When I look at paintings or pictures, I notice all the colors and shapes and how objects are spaced.

_____ I prefer learning from pictures.

_____ I picture things in my mind.

TOTAL _____

Intelligence #4

_____ I listen to music or have music playing in my head most of the time.

_____ I play a musical instrument and/or have a good singing voice.

_____ I can easily pick up rhythms and can move to them or tap them out.

_____ I can easily remember and/or create songs.

_____ I often make tapping sounds or sing while working or studying.

_____ I can remember things better if I put them in a song.

Taken from *The Co-Teaching Book of Lists*, by Katherine Perez. Copyright © 2012 by John Wiley & Sons, Inc.

_____ I can hear all the parts when I listen to music.

TOTAL _____

Intelligence #5

_____ Math is one of my favorite subjects.

_____ I like to play games such as chess, Clue, or Stratego.

_____ I like to do scientific experiments.

_____ I like to calculate, measure, and figure things out.

_____ I enjoy solving brain teasers and puzzles.

_____ Using a computer comes easily to me. I understand how they work and can spend time learning about them.

_____ I see patterns in things.

TOTAL _____

Intelligence #6

_____ I understand and can express my feelings

_____ I enjoy spending time by myself.

_____ I like to work alone.

_____ I am comfortable having ideas and opinions that are not the same as others.

_____ I feel good about who I am most of the time.

_____ I have a realistic view of my strengths and weaknesses.

_____ I enjoy playing games and doing activities that I can do by myself.

TOTAL _____

Intelligence #7

_____ I have many friends.

_____ I enjoy playing group games and group sports.

_____ I enjoy working in groups and tend to be the leader in the group.

_____ I really care about others and try to understand how others feel and think.

_____ I feel comfortable being in the middle of groups or crowds.

_____ I enjoy teaching another person or group of people something that I know how to do well.

_____ I like to get involved in social activities in school, church, or the community.

TOTAL _____

Intelligence #8

_____ I like to watch and observe what is going on around me.

_____ I think about the environment a lot and want to make sure that we don't pollute our planet.

_____ I like to collect rocks, leaves, and other items in nature.

_____ I feel best when I am out in nature.

_____ I understand how different plants and animals are connected to each other.

_____ I can easily get used to being in new places.

_____ I like to organize things and put them in categories.

TOTAL _____

Source: Adapted from K. Kryza, *Practical Inclusion Strategies: Maximizing Student Success in the Inclusive Classroom (Grades 6–12)* (Bellevue, WA: Bureau of Education and Research, 2007).

	Word Smart	Math Smart	Art Smart	Body Smart	Nature Smart	Self Smart	People Smart	Music Smart
10								
9								
8								
7								
6								
5								
4								
3								
2								
1								
0								

Chapter 7

Schoolwide Organization: Administrative Issues

List 7.1   Schoolwide Issues

Identifying Diverse Learners

- Who are the diverse learners at our school?
- What are their learning characteristics?
- How is our staff currently doing in meeting their needs?
- Which learners present a challenge to our staff?

Reflecting on Our Beliefs

- How do we ensure that all students learn?
- Why are some students not successful at learning?
- How competent are we in meeting the individual needs of our learners?
- Is the learning in our school teacher-directed or student-centered?

Identifying Our Competencies

- What strategies do we use that support differentiated learning?
- What instructional strategies do we use with our successful students?
- How might these same strategies be modified for use with the diverse learners in our classroom?
- What additional strategies do we need to support all learners?

Analyzing Structures for Co-Teaching

- What structures are currently in place that will enhance co-teaching?
- What barriers do we face in moving forward with co-teaching?

The Co-Teaching Book of Lists

List 7.2   Barriers to Successful Co-Teaching

At the school-site level, there are many barriers to overcome as you prepare to move toward a co-teaching program. Some of these obstacles are administrative in nature, others involve all staff at your school site, and some pertain only to the co-teaching team. Some of the barriers to consider and discuss are:

- Lack of professional development
- Negative previous experience with co-teaching at another site
- Inability or unwillingness to work with colleagues having different personalities or philosophies
- Reluctance to losing control of classroom and curriculum
- Lack of willingness to invest time and effort
- Lack of teacher knowledge and skill in:
  - Classroom management
  - Research-based instruction
  - Authentic assessment methods
  - Varying the instructional methods used
  - Interpreting student data for evaluation
- School culture issues
  - Emphasis on teacher competition or individuality
- No shared goals
- Limited shared resources
- Only individual accountability
- Rigid hierarchy among staff
  - Lack of equality and parity
  - Lack of mutual respect and trust
- Limited human and/or material resources
  - Scheduling issues
  - Common planning time
- Lack of administrative support or understanding
- Lack of parental understanding and support

List 7.3   Professional Development Issues

- Professional development should occur in a tiered and ongoing process before co-teaching is implemented
- The first phase of teacher-centered professional development is to engage the entire staff in an overview of the purpose and process of co-teaching
- In the initial phase, teachers are provided with techniques for differentiating content, process, and product in their classrooms and addressing the needs of all their diverse learners
- Teachers need to be reminded that these techniques are effective not only in co-teaching students with identified special needs, but also in meeting the individual needs of other students
- The next phase of professional development should include the co-teaching teams to enhance collaboration skills and focus on the models and various approaches to co-teaching
- Professional development is most effective when there is sustained contact over time that involves coaching, demonstration, observation, follow-up, and additional resources
- Administrative support is essential for professional development to be shared continuously throughout the year

Next are some additional suggestions to enhance the staff development efforts at your school site.

Critical Components of Professional Development for Co-Teaching

- Structured opportunities over time to develop mutual goals
- A forum to develop shared classroom rules, procedures, and routines
- Time to discuss and agree on initial roles and responsibilities
- Opportunities to collaboratively plan how to maximize classroom space
- Knowledge and skill in collaborative planning
- Knowledge and skill in developing multiple approaches to collaborative instruction
- Using the following to mitigate the effects of different personality types and learning styles on the co-teaching partnership:
  - Communication
  - Problem solving
  - Decision making
- Structured opportunities for reflection and continuous improvement
- Developing shared goals
  - Articulating shared goals early in the partnership provides direction and purpose for team members
  - Shared goals offer a measure of accountability and professional growth
  - Shared goals build the bond between the co-teachers

List 7.4   Scheduling Issues

- Which kinds of schedules exist in your school?
- How are these schedules determined?
- Is there an integrated, shared process of decision making when interfacing schedules?
- Does your school plan proactively for co-teaching implementation?

Scheduling Tips for Co-Teaching

- Begin the co-teaching process by considering:
  - A team of willing teachers
  - Number of students with identified needs
  - Levels of intensity of student need
- Co-teaching blocks should be scheduled for a minimum of forty-five minutes per classroom
- When designing schedules, try to limit the specialist's blocks of co-teaching time to three to four per day to maximize teachers' time and expertise
- For every block of co-teaching time, schedule at least forty-five minutes a week of planning time
- Co-teaching scheduling options to consider are:
  - Full-time co-teaching partnership
  - Part-time arrangements, with one to four different co-teachers for three to five days per week
  - Alternate days for an extended period of time, rather than every day for a short time
  - The specialist can be scheduled as part of a core subject team and then can rotate for students with similar needs
  - The specialist can be part of a department team and plan with them
- Time also needs to be allocated for other responsibilities such as assessment, IEP updates and meetings, materials modification, and consultations

List 7.5   Effective Methods for Placing Students

- Make well-informed decisions and hand-pick students to be placed in specific co-taught classrooms

- Make a conscious effort to consider certain student combinations; for instance, don't place several students with moderate to severe disabilities in the same classroom as students with behavior problems

- Look at the entire composition of the co-taught classroom to inform your decisions, so that advanced learners and students with special needs are somewhat balanced

- Consider other support services that the students may receive; for instance, you won't want to place several students who need to be pulled out for speech therapy in the same class, as this will only fragment their curriculum further

Taken from *The Co-Teaching Book of Lists*, by Katherine Perez. Copyright © 2012 by John Wiley & Sons, Inc.

The Co-Teaching Book of Lists

List 7.6 Techniques for Classroom Caseloads

When developing the schedules and placement of students for your co-taught classrooms at your school site, several factors need to be considered.

- You should agree on some basic principles that will guide the design of the schedules in your school—as a school team, with administrative support
- First look at each student individually, with his or her own unique needs
- Create a large grid or chart with the classes listed by grade level (elementary) or by subject area and period (secondary)
- Focus in on core subjects

  Elementary: language arts and math

  Secondary: English, math, science, and history
- Use color-coded sticky notes to represent each student to be placed
- Decide on the current readiness levels of the students to be placed

Sample Chart Looking at Student Needs

- High need: few independent work habits; reads one to two years below grade level
- Medium need: student functions OK, but is not self-motivated and will need some help with directions and completing tasks
- Low need: needs some monitoring; has difficulty organizing information; distracted
- Decide whether any of the students also have behavior problems and concerns, and code these with a dot on their sticky note

When you are determining each teacher's caseload, distribute the students on a chart like the one offered here for a wide view of your class grouping and co-teaching staffing decisions.

	K	1	2	3	4	5	6
Language arts							
Math							

List 7.7   Guiding Principles

- Establish common goals to develop your master schedule
  - ○ Maximize instructional time
  - ○ Maximize support for students
- Foster collaboration among staff for planning
- Take a noncategorical approach to service delivery that springs from student identified needs, not necessarily from students' special education "labels"
- All staff should participate and take ownership of all students to create the best programs at their grade levels
- Offer a continuum of service delivery options based on the needs of the students
- Base your scheduling decisions on maximizing student's success at accessing the general education curriculum
- Decide on regular time blocks for core subjects, if possible, to maximize the specialist's time; for instance, reading and math can be taught at the same time across grade levels, especially at elementary sites
- Collaborative planning should be scheduled occur at least once a week

List 7.8   Student Study Teams: A Pre-Referral Strategy

Student study teams (SSTs) are school-based problem-solving groups whose purpose is to assist general education teachers, administrators, and other school support staff with possible interventions for students who are facing academic challenges or who have social-emotional needs.

They meet on a regular basis to brainstorm possible interventions and creative ways to use available resources to assist the students being referred. SSTs not only meet the individual needs of the students, but also enhance the co-teaching programs with additional ideas in meeting the diverse needs of the learners.

SSTs are designed to:

- Meet a broader range of students in the greater instructional program
- Utilize group problem-solving skills to resolve academic and behavioral concerns
- Assist teacher sin modifying instructional strategies
- Provide positive behavioral supports for the classroom
- Reduce the number of inappropriate referrals to special education evaluation
- Identify early intervention techniques for students who may be at risk
- Promote a student-centered focus at the school site, not a content-focused perspective
- Seek out additional resources in the community and district
- Foster positive relationships with parents and community resources
- Develop a sense of teamwork and collaborative discussion among staff
- Enhance job-embedded professional development by sharing differing perspectives and expertise

Source: Adapted from M. Radius and P. Lesniak, *Student Study Teams: A Resource Manual for Trainers and Implementors, rev. ed.* (Sacramento, CA: Resources in Special Education, 1988).

List 7.9   Student Study Team Guidelines

Referring Teacher Preparation

The referring teachers will be aware that the other team members will expect them to have background information.

Materials you need to bring to the SST meeting:

1. Cumulative folder
   - Pre-SST worksheet
   - Student information form
   - Student profile
   - Parent input form
2. Recent work samples
   - Spelling
   - Reading
   - Math
   - Language arts

Be ready to discuss the following:

1. Reason for referral and a specific statement of the problem or problems
2. Areas of student strengths and weaknesses; academic skills

   Examples: Good in mathematics, loves to do handwriting, enjoys art, good in sports, difficult time reading textbooks, unable to phonetically sound out words, poor handwriting
3. Classroom behavior: peer relationships, adult relationships, and work habits

   Examples: Very cooperative, willing to please, chosen by classmates to be a leader, doesn't complete work or turn it in, poor study skills, talks excessively
4. What do you expect to get out of this meeting?

List 7.10   Roles and Responsibilities of Team Members

Team Member	Suggested Roles and Responsibilities
Principal or vice principal or administrator	Team leader Determines team constellation Calls team meetings Guides and directs discussion; facilitates problem-solving process during meetings Establishes time lines Insures that team decisions are properly implemented Functions as a liaison between school and community (for example, interprets concept of multidisciplinary teaming for school faculty and parents) Ensures implementation of appropriate procedures for identification, placement, programming, and evaluation of exceptional students
Classroom teacher(s)	Is primarily responsible for designing student's educational program in the regular classroom Is responsible for initial referral of students or assists other referring agent Is able to identify and collect information on students in classroom who may be potential candidates for special education services Is accountable to the team for recommendations implemented in the regular classroom Maintains ongoing communication with other team members regarding a particular student's program Serves as an advocate for the student in the regular classroom
Parents or legal guardians	Is the primary advocate for the student May initiate a referral for the student Ensures that the student receives an appropriate education Provides team with information regarding student's performance outside of school Maintains ongoing communication with the team regarding student's performance Provides input related to design of student's total educational program May implement and follow through with team recommendations in the home setting Must provide written consent for evaluations conducted by the team Must provide written consent for any changes in student's placement (such as resource rooms and special classes)

Team Member	Suggested Roles and Responsibilities
Resource teacher or special education teacher or educational diagnostician	Selects, administers, and interprets appropriate assessment instruments, including formal and informal measures of student performance May observe student in the regular classroom setting Compiles, organizes, and maintains files on students receiving special education services Designs programming alternatives for students using the assessment information collected May implement programs for the student Assists in coordination of student's total program Maintains ongoing records that reflect student's current performance levels Assists regular classroom teacher in modification and adaptation of curriculum May design and construct materials to meet the specific needs of exceptional students Can locate additional human and material resources that may be necessary for optimum functioning of team Maintains functional and current knowledge of curriculum materials Is accountable to the team for implantation of recommendations Maintains ongoing communication with other team members regarding a particular student's performance
Psychologist	Selects, administers, and interprets appropriate psychological, educational, and behavioral assessment instruments May observe student's performance in the regular classroom Assists in design and implementation of behavioral management programs in school and at home May consult and counsel with parents, teachers, and team members regarding student's cognitive, affective, and psychomotor development
Communication specialist or speech therapist	Selects, administers, and interprets appropriate diagnostic instruments designed to assess student's speech development, language development, and auditory perceptual skills May assist in design and implementation of speech, language, and auditory perceptual programs with individuals and groups of students May consult with parents, teachers, and other team members regarding speech and language problems

(continued)

Team Member	Suggested Roles and Responsibilities

School counselor	May take responsibilities similar to those listed under social worker
	
	Additional responsibilities (particularly at secondary level) may include the following:
	
	    May assist students in selection of classes and coordination of class schedules
	
	    May assist and counsel students regarding vocational decisions
	
	    May consult and counsel with students, parents, teachers, and other team members regarding such things as attendance, behavioral, and academic problems

School nurse	Collects and interprets relevant medical information for team members regarding student's health (such as screening for vision and hearing problems, conferring with physicians, or monitoring medications) Assists in management of chronically ill students in school setting Consults with parents, students, and other team members regarding short-term medical health needs of students (such as nutritional problems or childhood diseases)

List 7.11   How Administrators Can Support Co-Teaching

- Administrative support is a necessary and important ingredient for a successful co-teaching program at a school site
- Effective co-teaching is the result of committed teachers who are willing to collaborate and share their talents and time to help all students succeed
- There are many challenges to developing and sustaining a co-teaching program

Following are some things for administrators to keep in mind to support co-teaching and scheduling of students with special needs:

- Facilitate discussions for greater collaboration and to support team building
- Develop flexible schedules with teacher input and common planning times in mind
- Allow co-teachers to stay together for more than one year
- If possible, begin the process with teachers who are willing to participate instead of those who are reluctant
- Provide ongoing professional development with sustained support, observation, coaching, and follow-up over the academic year
- Make sure there are adequate resources to support the program and the curriculum modifications needed
- Develop the co-teaching program at your site gradually—one step at a time, one teacher at a time (perhaps start with a pilot program to discuss merits and challenges)
- Engage teachers in ongoing discussions of what is working, what is not working, and how they can modify the program
- Be sure to involve all staff in the development process of the co-teaching program
- Include para-educators as important professionals with specific roles and responsibilities in the co-teaching classroom
- Encourage teachers to observe and meet with other co-teachers in the district
- Encourage student-based decision-making
- Share with parents about the co-teaching program and the benefits for their students
- Involve parents in the process and have them share their impressions of the program by completing a survey
- Involve the entire staff in the master scheduling process, including specialists and support staff: this needs to be a schoolwide effort to support collaborative planning time and instructional blocks for co-teaching
- Grade-level teams need common planning time at the elementary level, and department teams need common planning time at the secondary level

List 7.12   Other Ways Administrators Can Support the Co-Teaching Team

Collaboration is a time-consuming process. Administrators might want to honor the efforts of the co-teachers in recognition of their dedication. Here are some possible positive pointers:

- Acknowledge them at the staff meeting
- Provide extra resources for adaptive materials
- Give them their choice of planning time
- Release them from traditional duties (recess or lunch duty) to provide them additional planning time
- Provide them with a larger classroom (if possible) that is more conducive to flexible grouping patterns and station teaching
- Have them do a presentation at a staff meeting about the benefits of co-teaching and share some successful curriculum modification strategies

List 7.13   Observing Co-Teachers

In addition to the Co-Teaching Observation Form at the end of this chapter, there are other indicators that administrators can use when observing co-teachers to provide them with more focused feedback. Here are some ideas:

- What approach to co-teaching did you observe?
- Were both teachers actively involved in the instructional process?
- What grouping patterns did you observe?
- Was the instruction differentiated? If so, did you observe evidence of differentiated content, process, or product?
- What examples of modification of materials or accommodation of instruction did you observe?
- How did the teachers relate to each other during instruction? How did they relate to the students?
- In what ways were the teachers each sharing their expertise with students?
- Are there extended learning opportunities for students to support visual, auditory, and kinesthetic learning styles?
- How was time used effectively?
- Was there evidence of clearly defined procedures and routines?
- What suggestions would you make to the teachers?

List 7.14 Providing Feedback

After the observation, the administrator should elicit the teachers' feedback first.

- Ask the teachers what worked. What didn't work? What would they do differently?
- Ask about the physical structure of the classroom environment—was it conducive to collaboration and flexible grouping?
- How has their teaching changed as a result of co-teaching? Discuss the implications on their practice.
- Ask for specific examples that show how they are meeting the diverse and unique needs of the students
- What would they change if they were to reteach the lesson?
- What are their next steps? Do they have an action plan?
- What practices do they want to improve?
- In what areas do they need additional support?
- Are they willing to share their experiences and strategies with other staff members? With parents?

Source: Adapted from M. Friend, *Co-Teach! A Handbook for Creating and Sustaining Successful Classroom Partnership in Inclusive Schools* (Greensboro, NC: MFI, 2008).

List 7.15   Co-Teaching Observation Form

Teacher names _____

Content _____ Special education _____

Subject _____ Date _____

Start time _____ End time _____ Debrief time _____ Other _____

Time	Instructional Materials	Instructional Methods or Co-Teaching Approach	Student Skills Request	Co-Teacher Role (Instructing or Assisting)	Student Behavior and Number Engaged	Comments Questions

Instructional Methods: Small Group (SG), Whole Group (WG), Individualized (I), or Varied (V)

Co-teaching approaches: One Teach, One Support (1), Station (ST), Parallel (P), Alternative (A), or Team (T)

Use a separate piece of paper to diagram the classroom and provide feedback on structure or engagement.

Taken from *The Co-Teaching Book of Lists*, by Katherine Perez. Copyright © 2012 by John Wiley & Sons, Inc.

The Co-Teaching Book of Lists

Chapter 8

Accommodations and Modifications That Make a Difference

List 8.1   What Are Accommodations, Modifications, and Interventions?

Accommodations: Changing *How* Students Access Curriculum

- Do not change integrity of the task
- Do not change basic instruction
- May have an impact on assessment
- May result in changing the delivery of instruction
- Do not mean additional services

Modifications: Changing *What* the Student Learns

- May affect the length of the assignment
- May change the level of difficulty of material
- May change approach to grading
- May alter the quantity of material to be mastered
- May have an impact on the assessment process
- May influence the pacing of instruction
- May change the complexity of questioning and higher-level thinking skills

Interventions: Changing *How* Instruction Is Delivered

- Different curriculum
- Different teaching and learning strategies
- Smaller-group instruction
- Direct, explicit skill instruction

List 8.2   Modification Versus Differential Standard

- In the spirit of the least restrictive environment and the individual education plan (IEP), instruction needs to be designed that appropriately accommodates the student's level of functioning and style of learning
- Students with special needs, as well as some of their general education peers, will benefit and gain greater access to the curriculum as a result of implementation
- The modification procedures should be described in the student's IEP
- A *modification* or *accommodation* occurs in the classroom when the learning outcome or instructional goal remains the same, but the student's path to get there and/or the methods of assessing or evaluating the learning are modified. Some examples include:
  - Taking the test orally
  - Extended time for taking the test
  - Getting hard copies of class notes to study
  - Limiting the quantity of homework assignments

The key here is that the learning standard remains the same; only the pathway to get there is changed. These kinds of modifications should be used in the general education classroom to maximize the student's learning potential.

Some modifications to consider:

- **Size:** limit the number of items or the quantity of text student is responsible for
- **Level of support:** increase the amount of assistance provided (through paraprofessionals, peers, cross-age tutors, and the like)
- **Time:** modify the amount of time allocated for lessons, assignments, or assessment
- **Instruction:** modify the delivery of instruction (for example, more hands-on, visual prompts, books on tape, and cooperative groups)
- **Difficulty:** modify the level of difficulty of the task to be accomplished

A *differential standard* suggests that the outcome or learning goal has been modified or is different from the expectations of the rest of the class. *This kind of modification needs to be written into the IEP* in order to be compliant.

Some examples might include:

- Student's grade is based on degree of improvement
- Standards of the product required for lesson are simplified
- Assess the student on key concepts only

Adaptations and Enhancements

These techniques enhance and extend the learning of all students—especially lower-performing students. They require teachers to make instructional changes in the curriculum. Adaptations and enhancements are designed to improve the learning outcomes and are very worthwhile to consider. Some examples include:

- Concept attainment
- Guided and paired reading

- Metacognitive instruction
- Graphic organizers
- Learning strategy instruction
- Reciprocal teaching
- Structured cooperative learning

When accommodations and/or modifications are used in the classroom, it is important to record the techniques and the outcome with the students. The chart in List 8.3 is an excellent record-keeping tool for keeping track of these strategies and their results.

List 8.3　Accommodations and Modifications Log

Student _____ Grade _____

Teacher _____

Date	Content	Activity	Accommodations and Modification (see key below)

Key for Accommodations and Modifications

1. Input modified (describe)
2. Quantity of work
3. Content modified
4. Student responds orally
5. Level of difficulty adjusted
6. Time

7. Behavioral adaptations
8. Small-group instruction
9. Level of support
10. Participation
11. Other:

   _____

The Co-Teaching Book of Lists

List 8.4 Accommodations or Modifications?

Accommodations: instructional practices that enable special needs students to acquire, retain, and demonstrate knowledge and understanding of content. Students are expected to learn the same content, and teachers maintain the same instructional goals. Some examples:

- Extended time
- Preteaching
- Oral directions
- Use of calculator or other adaptive devices

Modifications: significant changes made to the curriculum that enable a student to be successful in the general education classroom. Modifications change the curriculum objectives in some way. Some examples:

- The quantity of reading, written work, and the like are reduced
- Modifications reflect the educational rights of the student and should be included in the IEP
- Changes in grading procedures should be indicated on the report card; refer to your school district's policies

Accommodations and Modifications That Make a Difference

List 8.5   Adapting Instruction Flow Chart

When adapting instruction, keep in mind the steps in this flow chart.

A Decision-Making Approach

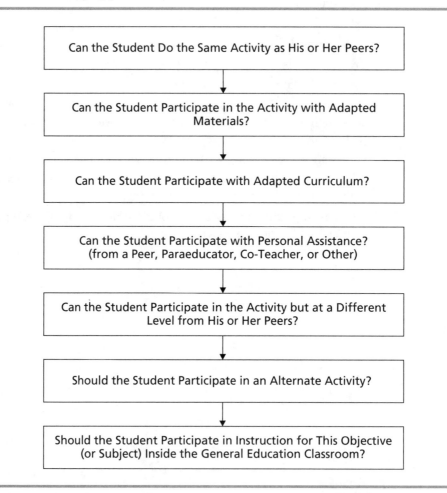

Source: Reprinted with permission from Stetson and Associates (www.stetsonassociates.com).

Taken from *The Co-Teaching Book of Lists*, by Katherine Perez. Copyright © 2012 by John Wiley & Sons, Inc.

The Co-Teaching Book of Lists

List 8.6   Planning Guide to Curriculum Modifications

Determine what you want the students to know, understand, and be able to do as a result of the lesson

Preassess—how will you determine their current level of understanding before starting your lesson?

What will be most challenging for some learners to understand?

How might you differentiate the content, process, or product of the lesson?

What modifications will be most helpful to your struggling students?

In what ways will you set the stage for learning, build background knowledge, and engage the learners to create a need to know?

How can you and your co-teacher work together to modify and deliver the instruction to the students?

Modifying Input and Output of Information

- How will students *take in* the information?
  - Hearing the information from teacher or recorded tapes
  - Through a hands-on experience to gain information
  - Viewing the new information through pictures or charts
  - Reading information from text, online, or the like
- How will the student *process* the information?
  - Manipulating objects to represent information learned
  - Talking: sharing with another about the new information
  - Using graphic organizers to connect content being learned
  - Doing a quick-write activity to capture main ideas
- How will you *check for understanding* and transfer of learning?
  - Provide student with different projects that show their understanding
    * Build a model
    * Make a video
    * Create a poem
    * Act out a scene; bring the lesson to life
  - Have students select from a range of questions about the text to show what they know
  - Offer various projects for students to choose from according to their readiness to assess learning

Reflection

- What worked in the lesson?
- What would you change for next time?
- What about monitoring, management, and grouping strategies?

List 8.7   Modifications "On the Move"

Co-Teacher's Toolbox Tote

Many times you find yourself in a position to modify on the go. To help with flexible fix-it strategies, each co-teacher should be equipped with a lightweight, portable toolbox. The contents of your toolbox may vary, depending on the age and ability level of your students. Here are some suggested items to pack to get you started:

- Clipboard
- Sticky notes
- Index cards
- Highlighters
- Portable (disposable) camera
- Paper clips
- Rubber bands
- Envelopes
- Pencil grips
- Mini flashlights
- Graph paper
- Colored pens and pencils
- Highlighter tape
- Magnifying glass
- Scissors
- Dice
- Deck of cards (for grouping)
- Stickers

List 8.8   Co-Teacher Communication Cards

Often in a co-taught classroom, events and learning experiences happen at a very fast pace. Why not keep track of those good co-teaching ideas along the way? Record those good ideas or unexpected roadblocks encountered on a simple three-by-five card to give valuable feedback to your co-teacher.

- Which modifications worked best? Why?
- What pitfalls have you encountered?
- What would you do differently? Why?
- Ongoing communication with your co-teacher is essential to your partnership
- Don't make assumptions
- Don't reinvent the wheel
- Keep an open mind

Following is a sample communication card to help get the ideas flowing.

Co-Teacher Communication Card

This worked great: _____

_____

I noticed: _____

_____

Next time let's try this: _____

_____

This did not work so well: _____

_____

List 8.9   Checklist of Accommodations and Modifications

Classroom Environment

- Get close to student when giving directions
- Seat student up front near the teacher and the board
- For students who are highly distractible and have attention problems, use a study carrel (made of trifold cardboard from office supply store)
- Arrange classroom for greater visibility, accessibility, movement, and flexibility

Giving Lectures and Presenting Lessons

- Provide visual reinforcement (charts, posters, graphs, and overheads)
- Provide written backup to oral directions
- Give student an outline or study guide to follow as an advance organizer
- Highlight the instructions
- Ask student to repeat instructions to you or to another student for greater clarity
- Give clear and concise objectives
- Pause and question throughout the lesson
- Engage students in sharing with learning partners what they learned at frequent intervals
- Use flash cards or cards with key concepts
- Give explanations in small, sequenced steps
- Alternate verbal directions with written tasks for greater comprehension
- Interject humor and stories
- Preteach key vocabulary and concepts
- Do an activator strategy to engage students and to tap into their background knowledge about the topic
- Repeat important ideas throughout the lecture, pausing to check for comprehension

Presentation of Lessons

- Adjust student workload, reduce the number of assignments, or give a choice of alternate assignment related to objectives
- Provide clear objectives and outcomes
- Explain evaluation criteria for the lesson
- Use hands-on materials to demonstrate lesson
- Positively acknowledge students' efforts often
- Remind students to stay on task and focus

Note-Taking Strategies

- Provide student with a copy of lecture notes with key ideas highlighted
- Allow student to tape-record lessons and discussions
- Arrange for another student to be a note-taker

Taken from *The Co-Teaching Book of Lists*, by Katherine Perez. Copyright © 2012 by John Wiley & Sons, Inc.

- Teach students note-taking strategies
- Have students discuss main ideas with learning partners
- Allow time for periodic review of notes

Organizational Techniques

- Have student keep assignment notebook and calendar of assignment due dates
- Develop a daily schedule for the student or at least an agenda for your class
- Have a check-in time at the beginning of the day to get organized
- Develop a parent-school communication log and/or contract
- Provide skill-building sessions on time management
- Give sessions on test-taking skills

Layout of Written Materials

- Is the material clear and visually appealing?
- Can students read it easily or do you need to enlarge the type?
- Avoid a crowded worksheet—is there adequate white space?
- Divide worksheets into sections for specific types of problems
- Is there too much text on the page?
- Is the text sharp and clear?
- Are there multiple activities and tasks on one page?
- Offer several choices for the format of projects (not just written reports)
- Use a gamelike format to navigate text

Textbook Considerations

- Use supplemental informational texts that are more accessible
- Obtain textbooks on tape from Learning Ally (formerly Recordings for the Blind)
- Provide prediction questions in advance
- Have students look at headings and turn them into questions to stimulate a need to know
- Shorten the amount of required reading
- Allow students extra time for reading text
- Demonstrate skimming and scanning techniques
- Have students use sticky notes so they can code their text as they read and flag VIPs (very important points). Use plastic report covers to cover pages of text and provide student with erasable markers to underline a focus or key ideas

Content Issues

- Limit the number of problems or examples per page
- Is all the material necessary?
- Arrange problems appropriately on page with adequate space between items

- Do not give students multiple assignments at once—just one direction or assignment at a time
- Is the reading level appropriate?
- Is the content presented in small segments? How can you adjust for that?
- Have students create a word bank of key vocabulary words before the reading
- Are the objectives clear?
- Does the content focus on the students' strengths and learning style?

Directions

- Does each section have different directions and specific examples?
- Are the directions clear and concise?
- Is the sentence structure simple and straightforward?
- Do the students understand the language and terms used?
- Are the steps appropriate to the student's readiness level?

Grouping Structures

- Peer tutoring
- Learning partners
- Small groups
- Study buddy
- Cross-age tutoring
- Paraprofessional help
- Teach student to monitor his or her own behavior
- Implement independent study or behavior contract

Alternative Evaluation Procedures

- Use short, frequent quizzes
- Does the test begin with an easier question?
- Is performance assessment an option?
- Does the student have enough time to finish?
- Are there ways to differentiate the assessment? (Perhaps verbally, on tape, in a different location, or at a different time?)
- Reduce the number of test items
- Arrange for verbal testing
- Practice taking similar test questions with a similar format
- What kinds of questions are used? Recall? Recognition? Inference?
- Have paraprofessional administer test
- Adjust grading criteria according to individual ability
- Adjust evaluation process to pass–not pass

Taken from *The Co-Teaching Book of Lists*, by Katherine Perez. Copyright © 2012 by John Wiley & Sons, Inc.

The Co-Teaching Book of Lists

List 8.10   Focus on Curriculum Adaptations

Accommodating the students' functional levels and learning style may involve the following adaptations.

- **Input:** modifying how the information is transmitted to the student; examples include visual aids, hands-on manipulatives, and audiotapes
- **Output:** modifying how the student communicates what he or she has learned; adapt according to students' response to instruction:
  - Instead of answering questions in writing, students have the choice to sing, draw, dance, act, or create a model of what they have learned
  - Read the test aloud to the student and have him or her respond verbally, instead of in writing
- **Quantity:** adapting the amount of work required of the student; change the number of items that the learner is expected to learn or complete:
  - Reduce the number of science terms a student learns from text; use key terms only
  - Do every other math problem for homework
- **Time:** modifying the amount of time the student has for task completion, learning, and testing:
  - Pace the learning differently for some students
  - Give students time and a half to take a test
  - Create an independent timeline for project completion
- **Difficulty:** adapt the skill level of the work to better meet the readiness level of the student:
  - Change the instructions to meet the needs of the student
  - Allow the student to use a calculator for computation
  - Simplify written and oral directions
- **Participation:** modify the level of the student's active involvement in a task or assignment:
  - Student may label a map while the class inserts capitals
  - Student may serve as moderator of a spelling bee and keep track of points instead of actively participating
  - Allow the student to move frequently during activities
- **Level of support:** students may need a different level of support and individual assistance to learn a concept:
  - Increase the amount of instructional support a student receives
  - Provide peer partner, paraprofessional, or cross-age tutors
- **Alternate goals:** modifying the level of difficulty of lesson while using the same curriculum content
  - While some students are outlining the main ideas of a chapter, the student draws sketches of key concepts on a storyboard

- **Substitute curriculum:** modifying content and process of assignment by providing different instruction and resource materials to meet individual student's goals
  - While a group of students explores sources for their research report in the library, other students may read text out loud with a paraprofessional
  - During a science test, student is refining his computer skills

List 8.11   Adaptation Application Activity

Instructions: Review these classroom examples and write the student name corresponding to the kind of adaptation that situation exemplifies under one of the nine adaptation application categories. Discuss with a small group and compare your responses.

The goal is to become familiar with the most commonly used adaptations and their application in a co-taught classroom.

- Linda completes a two-sentence summary of a story while the classmates write a three-paragraph essay.
- Mark learns his multiplication facts by January while the rest of the class learns them by November.
- Michael draws the life cycle of a butterfly while his classmates write reports on this natural phenomenon.
- Juanita has a learning partner in a cooperative learning task for history that keeps her on task and focused.
- Agnes points to the correct math answer on a grid while her classmates give verbal responses.
- Latoya knows it is lunchtime when her teacher holds up a lunch ticket, while the classmates read the time on the daily agenda.
- Sam writes the beginning sound of the words in a spelling test while his classmates write the word in a sentence.
- Kevin takes his exam to his cross-age tutor so that he can read the test questions to him and Kevin responds verbally.
- Devon completes ten math problems while his classmates complete the entire worksheet for the homework.
- Kathy's role is to call out the student's name for a class discussion when the teacher points to a student to respond to a question.
- Tony works on matching skills and fluency on the computer while his classmates read about the Civil War.
- Sam listens to a book on tape while his classmates read the novel during sustained silent reading.
- Ashley passes out maps to the students while the classmates locate specific spots on the maps.
- Kim works on handwriting skills with the paraprofessional while the classmates work on graphic organizers summarizing a chapter.

Adaptation Applications

Quantity	Time	Level of Support
Input	Difficulty	Output
Participation	Alternate Goals	Substitute Curriculum

List 8.12   Strategies for Supporting Students with Special Needs in the General Education Classroom

Here are some ideas you might like to try in your co-teaching classroom. Check those that might be helpful to your students and add ideas of your own to share with your co-teacher.

Students with ADD or ADHD

- ❑ Create a structured, predictable environment
- ❑ Keep a daily schedule and provide the student with an assignment book to keep track of assignments
- ❑ "Catch them being good" and share positive comments
- ❑ Prepare the student for transitions with a clear signal
- ❑ Remove unnecessary distractions on their work area or desk
- ❑ Have the student keep a planner for due dates, assignments, and homework
- ❑ Allow brain breaks for the student about every ten to twelve minutes where you change the input or the output of information
- ❑ Be specific about classroom procedures and routines
- ❑ Provide frequent feedback on progress made by student
- ❑ Provide self-monitoring and self-evaluation strategies for student
- ❑ Be aware of any medications student may be taking, along with doses and potential side effects
- ❑ Establish eye contact often during the day and maintain it while speaking to the student
- ❑ Teach organizational skills
- ❑ Reinforce study skills
- ❑ Color-code notebooks for different subjects
- ❑ Develop individual behavior plans with clear expectations, feedback, and reinforcement
- ❑ Model the use of guided practice and application
- ❑ Make sure you teach conflict resolution skills and peer mediation techniques
- ❑ Use subtle, nonverbal cues for transitions
- ❑ Use proximity and make your verbal directions specific and clear

_____

_____

_____

Students with Behavior Disorders

- ❑ Expect the best from the student
- ❑ Focus on improving student's self-confidence and self-esteem through your positive attitude and actions

- ❑ Use independent behavior contracts with clear expectations and consequences
- ❑ Provide verbal and visual cues for the student—sign language signals may be helpful
- ❑ Focus on the antecedents of the problem behavior; what is the possible cause?
- ❑ Try to avoid certain "triggers" for the student in the classroom that might set him or her off
- ❑ Try charting frequency of desired behavior so that you can use positive reinforcement
- ❑ Use active listening techniques with student to show you are attentive to his or her needs
- ❑ Help the student develop strategies for self-monitoring his or her own behavior
- ❑ Make sure you have modeled conflict resolution techniques
- ❑ Teach the student techniques for positive social interaction with peers through the use of role play
- ❑ Establish regular and ongoing home and school coordination and communication
- ❑ Provide a definite structure with limits and consequences

_____

_____

_____

Students with Learning Disabilities

- ❑ Make sure student is well aware of classroom procedures and routines
- ❑ Provide a daily and weekly planner with a calendar indicating the day, week, and month of due dates and homework
- ❑ Help the student organize desk, supplies, backpack, and so on
- ❑ Allow extended time for student to complete tasks, assignments, and tests as needed
- ❑ Develop specific accommodations with your co-teacher for classwork and homework
- ❑ Collaboratively develop IEP with all individuals involved with student
- ❑ Use concrete and kinesthetic materials that student can see and touch
- ❑ Scaffold instruction into step-by-step lessons
- ❑ Use redundancy and repetition to insure retention
- ❑ Vary your instructional delivery to encourage more active engagement of the student
- ❑ Emphasize consistent expectations with appropriate accountability
- ❑ Maintain frequent parent communication and collaboration
- ❑ Shorten assignments according to demonstrated mastery
- ❑ Encourage independence by targeting students' appropriate readiness level
- ❑ Help students remember procedures through the use of rhyme, rhythm, rap, and the like

❏ Carefully sequence the delivery of instruction to help the student: preview, preteach, review, and reteach

❏ Provide written outline summaries of main ideas, study guides, and focus questions as advance organizers

❏ Provide various graphic organizers to allow student to retain main ideas

_____

_____

_____

Students with Autism or Asperger Syndrome

❏ Use visual aids for prompts to reinforce learning

❏ Keep classroom procedures and routines as consistent as possible

❏ Monitor student's program carefully

❏ Demonstrate and teach appropriate social and interaction skills through role-play

❏ Clearly communicate expectations for each assignment both verbally and visually and have students repeat directions for greater understanding

❏ Develop individual contracts to assist in task completion

_____

_____

_____

Students with Developmental Delays

❏ Repeat directions as needed

❏ Teach tasks and lessons in carefully scaffolded steps

❏ Be sure to sequence your instruction

❏ Be consistent about the student's role in the classroom

❏ Develop the student's independence as much as possible

❏ Check in frequently with the student for understanding

❏ Provide additional time and practice for skill development

❏ Focus on support and instruction in small steps and reinforce along the way

❏ Allow a longer response time to questions

❏ Have student work with a learning partner to increase understanding of concepts

❏ Teach specific strategies to enhance social skills and positive peer interaction

_____

_____

_____

Students with Physical Impairments

❏ Use technology with adaptive devices

❏ Adapt the physical environment of the classroom to meet students' mobility needs

❏ Designate a peer buddy to assist with some physical tasks

- ❑ Focus on strengths and interests of student
- ❑ Educate other students about misconceptions and acceptance—many resources are available among current children's literature
- ❑ Collaborate with other specialists to design an integrated program including speech therapist, physical therapist, and occupational therapist as needed
- ❑ Teach self-help skills for greater independence

_____
_____
_____

Students with Visual Impairments

- ❑ Support visual information with verbal instructions
- ❑ Consider adaptations in lighting
- ❑ Enlarge the print on handouts and worksheets with the copy machine
- ❑ Have student use mini flashlights to illuminate print on page for greater contrast and visibility
- ❑ Reduce unnecessary clutter in room
- ❑ Reduce amount of print on page by blocking off some of the work so student can focus better
- ❑ Provide more hands-on methods
- ❑ Gradually add difficulty and time of duration of visual tasks
- ❑ Use books on tape
- ❑ Use students' stronger modalities to support and enhance learning
- ❑ Use computers with talking text options
- ❑ Use highlighters and colored overlays
- ❑ Provide information in graphic organizer format for greater clarity
- ❑ Visually separate information provided

_____
_____
_____

Students with Communication Disorders

- ❑ Modeling is very important
- ❑ Coordinate with speech therapist on interventions used and development of classroom goals that are appropriate
- ❑ Use more visuals
- ❑ Categorize and sort words
- ❑ Use tape recorders
- ❑ Demonstrate patience and wait time—giving student adequate time to respond is important
- ❑ Use adaptive technology for nonspeaking students
- ❑ Practice consistently in classroom and coordinate with home for additional practice
- ❑ Use communication boards with pictures to facilitate communication

The Co-Teaching Book of Lists

- ❏ Use computer programs to link speech and writing
- ❏ Instruct through conversations—relate communication with student's personal experiences and interests

_____

_____

_____

List 8.13   A Closer Look at Special Needs Challenges and Choices for Co-Teaching

Language Impaired		Learning Disabled (Reading)	
Student may experience difficulty	*Needs*	*Student may experience difficulty*	*Needs*
Following directions	Use graphic organizers	Following directions	Use graphic organizers
Attending to a lecture	Use direct and active instruction of specific skills	Understanding what others mean	Use direct instruction of specific skills
Understanding questions	Model examples for student to follow	Understanding questions	Provide examples for student to follow
Processing oral directions	Break down longer tasks into smaller steps	Processing oral directions	Break down longer tasks into smaller steps
Understanding words	Give immediate feedback	Understanding words	Immediate feedback
Remembering what was said	Use index cards with examples of how to do problems	Remembering what was said	Use index cards with examples of how to do problems
Recalling information	Use charts or visuals on desk	Recalling information from past experiences	Use charts or visuals on desk
Retelling and summarizing stories	Use visual scheduling (with step-by-step to-do lists)	Retelling stories	Use visual scheduling (with step-by-step to-do lists)
Expressing ideas	Use alternative assessments (oral, videos, posters, and projects)	Expressing ideas	Use alternative assessments (oral, videos, posters, and projects)
Following directions	Work with learning partner for prompts	Thinking logically	Engage a peer tutor
Knowing how to begin a task and follow through to completion	Provide more opportunities for practice and repetition	Following directions	Provide more opportunities for practice and repetition
Learning new vocabulary		Knowing how to begin a task and how to go on from there	Provide a quiet place to focus without distractions
Decoding or recognizing words		Learning new vocabulary	
Remembering the sounds that letters make		Decoding or recognizing words	
Perceiving the correct order of letters in words		Remembering the sounds that letters make	
		Perceiving the correct order of letters in words	

Cognitively Impaired		Behavior and/orMotivational Issues	
Student may experience difficulty	*Needs*	*Student may experience difficulty*	*Needs*
Following directions Attending to a lecture Understanding social cues of others Understanding questions Processing oral directions Understanding words Remembering what was said Recalling information from past experiences Retelling and summarizing stories Expressing ideas Thinking logically Following directions Knowing how to begin a task and follow through to completion Learning new vocabulary	Use graphic organizers Use direct and active instruction of specific skills Model examples for student to follow Break down longer tasks into smaller steps Provide frequent and supportive feedback Use index cards with examples of how to do problems Place charts or visuals on desk Use visual scheduling (with step-by-step to-do lists) Use alternative assessments (oral, videos, posters, and projects) Have student work with a learning partner for prompts Offer more opportunities for practice and repetition	Completing a task Following directions Beginning to work Utilizing effective work habits or learning strategies	Let students choose the types of graphic organizer that work for them (recognize student strengths and make use of them in learning) Use direct instruction and peer coaching Provide opportunities for self-correction Encourage student to do goal setting and self-monitoring Use visual scheduling (with step-by-step to-do lists) Use and practice appropriate behavior patterns explicitly Use metacognitive questioning to encourage self-reflection such as, ''What is something that you were very good at today? How do you know that you did that well?''

Source: Adapted from the National Dissemination Center for Children with Disabilities (http://nichcy.org).

List 8.14   I Have a Student Who . . . : What to Do?

I Have a Student Who Has Problems Getting Started and Focusing on Work

- Have a peer buddy restate the directions to the student; then have the student paraphrase the directions and expectations in his or her own words
- Check in on the student's progress frequently at the start of a lesson
- Have the student use a small digital timer and chart his or her start time progress on a daily basis for reinforcement
- Give clear and concise directions, delineating one step at a time
- Relate the content to the student's background and life experience
- Use verbal and visual cues to get the student started
- Have the student ask clarifying questions before getting started
- Make sure worksheets are uncluttered and easy to read
- Give the student a checklist to verify that they have all needed materials for lesson
- Use proximity with the student and seat him or her near the front of the class
- Chunk the lesson into discernable segments

I Have a Student Who Has Trouble Getting His or Her Work Done

- Reduce the amount of work required if student can demonstrate competency regarding content
- Check in with the student regarding time left to complete assignment ("You have five more minutes before you need to turn in this assignment...")
- Help the student keep a planner with assignment due dates
- Use verbal and visual prompts for reinforcement
- Give the student two index cards to display on his or her desk—for example, green means go, and red indicates completion of assignment
- Set clear limits
- Allow student to respond into a tape player to be played back later
- Work with the parents for a collaborative arrangement and keep an extra set of texts at home
- Allow an extended time for completion (specified at onset of task)
- Replicate the questions to be answered on a worksheet so student only has to fill in the blanks, rather than rewriting the entire question
- Use a visual digital timer (not a buzzer) to keep student on task and focused
- Divide the workload, requiring only even or odd numbers to be completed
- Provide student with a checklist of procedures and routines to monitor his or her own progress
- Allow student to respond with a visual symbol or sketch instead of a written answer

Taken from *The Co-Teaching Book of Lists*, by Katherine Perez. Copyright © 2012 by John Wiley & Sons, Inc.

I Have a Student Who Has Trouble Taking Notes

- Allow the student to tape the lecture and listen to it later, playing it back at a slower speed and being able to pause it as needed
- Provide student with an advanced organizer that shows a framework of the key concepts to transcribe from the lesson
- If you take notes on the overhead or visualizer, provide student with a copy so they can fill in the gaps
- Preview key points of lecture and key vocabulary to increase comprehension
- Provide a copy of the teacher's notes so that the student can compare it to his or her own and highlight main ideas to remember
- Have a study buddy take notes for student on NCR paper (carbonless copy paper) to share
- Teach the student how to review by highlighting main ideas from the notes
- Have paraprofessional review student notes after lesson and see what else they might recall
- Teach common cue phrases and academic signal words that will help student organize his or her notes
- Teach common abbreviations that will make note taking much more efficient
- Help the student develop his or her own shorthand for taking notes
- Give student a partial outline of lecture to complete
- Allow student to actively listen to lesson and then summarize verbally with a learning partner before writing down key ideas

I Have a Student Who Has Trouble Taking Written Tests

- Provide hands-on approaches to showing what they know by providing sticky notes and allowing them to sequence their answers before responding
- Allow for an open-book test or let them use their notes
- Allow extended time
- Provide breaks during test time to increase student's focus and attention
- Restate the directions and have the student paraphrase them
- Provide some kind of place marker like an index card, so that student can keep their place on the test form
- Show student how to highlight certain key words on the test before starting to answer
- Break up long lists of questions into smaller chunks
- Allow student to write on the test instead of copying down all the questions
- Test in a small group or one-to-one situation
- Read the test out loud to the student
- Provide an opportunity to redo test to bring their grade up
- Allow student to dictate responses to essay questions on a tape recorder or to the paraprofessional and review them later
- Provide a word bank that will help students with responses
- Show the student models of exemplary tests from past students—what do they look like?

I Have a Student Who Has Trouble Staying on Task

- Set specific time limits to prepare students ("this assignment will be due in fifteen minutes...")
- Use proximity with student and move his or her seat to the front of the room
- Try to reduce distractions and clear student's work space
- Give frequent and positive feedback
- Help student become more independent and make his or her own checklists for task completion
- Use peer helpers or cross-age tutors
- Talk with student and agree on nonverbal cues or sign language as reminders for them to pay attention and stay focused
- Create every-pupil response cards to reply to questions and ensure engagement (such as Yes and No cards or cards numbered one through five for multiple-choice questions)
- Reduce the quantity of work provided
- Use a visual digital silent timer for target students to complete work
- Randomly call on students so that everyone needs to be attentive; write each student's name on Popsicle sticks or a deck of cards, then ask students to respond when their name comes up and allow them to pass if they do not know the answer
- Provide shortened tasks
- Vary activities often for greater engagement
- Allow student to move around as a "resource manager," to pass out papers, collect assignments, and so forth to keep them moving with a positive purpose
- For students who are highly distractible, use a study carrel (trifold cardboard carrels are available at office supply stores)

I Have a Student Who Has Trouble Expressing Himself in Writing

- Assist student in creating an outline for a written piece
- Help student brainstorm words related to topic
- Give specific steps and sequence for writing assignments
- Have students prepare a word bank of vocabulary they can use in the essay
- Have the student make a concept map of related ideas around a central theme before writing
- Request that student record his or her essay or story into a tape recorder to get ideas out and then convert the words to written expression later
- Create a framework or template of the structure of an essay and have the student fill in the blanks
- Have students write research facts on separate index cards, then arrange the ideas before they write the final report
- At the revision stage, help student by highlighting words or ideas that are similar in the same color, so that ideas may be grouped together in order for the final draft
- Keep a selection of pictures, photos, or postcards to use as writing prompts and to generate ideas

- For primary students who have fine motor problems, provide special paper with raised lines for writing
- Allow student access to a word processor for writing drafts
- Have student select his or her own writing topic for journal that day
- Have students illustrate the key points of their paper and then write captions to support them
- Provide students with writing software that helps organize their ideas
- Teach mnemonics or acronyms to help them remember the components of a finished composition:
  - COPS (capitalization, organization, punctuation, spelling)
  - SPACE (spelling, punctuation, appearance, capitalization, error analysis)

I Have a Student Who Has Trouble Spelling

- Have your student create a word book that serves as their personal dictionary; this could also take the form of an index card file of new words learned
- Have student watch you write the words then trace over your writing with a highlighter
- Try "screen spelling": cut medium-mesh aluminum screen into nine-by-twelve-inch rectangles and trim them with masking tape; when student puts paper on top of screen, writes word with crayon, and traces it with a finger, the screen provides a raised surface and a multi-kinesthetic approach to spelling
- For primary students, use other materials that provide tactile feedback to your student, such as shaving cream, pudding, sand, or cornstarch
- Shorten the spelling list by modifying the number of required words
- Teach the student to use an electronic speller
- Highlight to help student: base word, prefixes, and suffixes
- Develop parent-school partnership by sending home the spelling words for the semester to the parents with suggestions and adaptations to help them practice and reinforce the spelling with their child
- Provide an audiotaped recording of the spelling list for the student to listen and respond to
- Develop an individual spelling contract with the student, gradually increasing mastery required for the spelling words
- Use the vocabulary-self-selection technique: student chooses specific words that are meaningful to him or her, in addition to those on the list
- Have the student spell the words verbally instead of in writing
- Help the student by giving the number of sounds or letters in a word when testing

I Have a Student Who Has Trouble Keeping Track of Assignments and Materials for Class

- Use sticky notes to mark the assignments in the text or workbook
- Have the student keep an assignment book with tasks to be done, due date, and approximate time needed to complete assignment

- Help the student develop his or her own self-monitoring techniques to help them remember supplies and assignments
- In his or her assignment book, have student write a list of materials to remember
- After you give directions, have student repeat and paraphrase the materials needed
- Have student call home and leave a message on the answering machine stating the homework assignment for that night; when they get home, they play the message and get to work
- Write each assignment due on a separate sticky note; when a student completes an assignment, that note is thrown away
- Have students place remaining sticky notes of outstanding assignments that are not completed in a special folder in their desk or notebook for the class
- Develop a set of nonverbal cues or hand signals to help the student remember to self-check for materials and assignments
- Display a master calendar of due dates and materials needed for all of the class to monitor and view
- Develop a checking system so that you can initial in their assignment book when a task has been completed
- Post assignments in the same place in the classroom daily for students to copy; consistency is the key
- Keep an extra supply of necessary materials in the classroom in case of emergencies
- Develop a system to help the student break up the assignment into smaller steps toward completion
- Contact the parents about your policies regarding assignment completion and share with them the main due dates that are pending
- Pair the student with a study buddy to check in with daily upon arriving and/or before leaving class to make sure needed materials and assignments are at hand

The Co-Teaching Book of Lists

List 8.15   Modifications Based on Students' Learning Styles

Visual	Auditory	Kinesthetic or Tactile
Write directions on the overhead or board as well as giving them verbally	Record assignment directions on tape, so the student can replay them as needed	Use frequent classroom demonstration and participatory modeling
Give students a written copy of weekly assignments	Give verbal as well as written directions	Allow student to build models, draw pictures, or make a display instead of writing reports
Use highlighters and highlighting tape	Get textbook materials on tape for the student to listen to while reading	Use role-play and simulations
Make or have students make study cards in bold colors	Use noisemakers to get attention	Provide a presentation outline for student
Create a pictorial behavior contract	Audiotape directions to play later	Play sound ball: throw information around room
Use symbolic summaries to sketch main ideas	Develop a song about the information	Model and scaffold note taking
Supplement presentations with digital slides or colorful transparencies, and use models, charts, graphs, and other visual aids	Have student leave assignment on home answering machine	Allow the student to move about during class
	Tape student reading and then replay it	Use sticky notes to capture main ideas
Have students use mini flashlights for reading along in texts	Allow student to sit in quiet space in room	Give students something to ''fidget'' with while learning
	Give an oral rather than written test	Use a beach ball summary
Use graphic organizers	Allow student to use a tape recorder to recite and then play back	Use screen spelling with a crayon for tactile stimulation
Give visual signals to students that it is their turn to be called on	Allow student to practice aloud with another student	Use magnets on cookie sheets or file cabinets
Allow students to read assignments, rather than depending on oral presentations	Substitute oral reports or other projects for written assignments	Use manipulative objects when teaching abstract concepts such as fractional parts, measurement, or geometry
Allow written reports or projects, rather than oral ones	Have another student read important information	Use Velcro boards on carpet squares for spelling and math
Teach students to take notes on important words, concepts, and ideas	Allow student to use headphones to block out noise	Set up hopscotch with facts instead of numbers
Color-code different subjects	Drill facts out loud	Use standing workstations
		Have student stand to answer

Accommodations and Modifications That Make a Difference

List 8.16   Adaptations and Modifications Chart

Subject: Period: Grade:									
Student Initials									
Modify format by:									
Enlarging font									
Adding charts									
Adding pictures									
Using concrete models									
Providing books on tape									
Illustrating notes and flash cards									
Color-coding study materials									
Providing word banks									
Providing memory maps									
Flowcharting process									
Using print versus cursive									
Using picture stories and visual directions									
Providing an outline									
Highlighting key points									
Moving from word lists to index cards									

Taken from *The Co-Teaching Book of Lists*, by Katherine Perez. Copyright © 2012 by John Wiley & Sons, Inc.

Subject:	Period:		Grade:							
Student Initials										
Providing opportunity to respond orally										
Emphasizing major points (use AutoSummarize tool)										
Providing study carrel for focus										
Tape-recording required reading for student										
Providing braille										
Adapt instruction by teaching with:										
Illustrated notes and handouts										
Color-coded teaching materials										
Memory maps										
Mnemonics										
Hands-on activities										
Assignment notebooks										
Frequent and/or immediate feedback										
Adapt assignments by providing:										
Simplified directions										
Memory aides										

(*continued*)

Accommodations and Modifications That Make a Difference

Subject:	Period:				Grade:					
Student Initials										
Silly rhymes to remember										
Re-worded text										
Material with reduced reading difficulty										
Reduced quantity										
Taped quantity										
Special projects in lieu of assignments										
Opportunity to leave class for assistance										
Opportunity to repeat and explain instructions										
Auditory aids (such as tapes)										
Extra time for oral response										
Extra time for written response										
Exams of reduced length										
Oral tests										
A scribe										
Peer tutoring										
Other										

									← **Student Initials**
									Tests: retake
									Tests: extra time
									Tests: oral
									Tests: modified
									Tests: scribe
									Write assignments on board
									Monitor assignments notebook
									Break down assignments into steps
									Provide copies of notes
									Substitute hands-on for written
									Substitute oral for written
									Seating preference
									Allow word processor
									Allow calculator
									Allow text-to-speech software
									Allow speech-to-text software

(continued)

Accommodations and Modifications That Make a Difference

									← **Student Initials**
									Provide advanced organizer
									Provide one-to-one assistance
									Visual cues and hands-on critical
									Easily overwhelmed
									Distractible
									Written expression weak
									Verbal expression weak
									Auditory learner
									Visual learner
									Kinesthetic learner

Download a digital version of this form at www.aimhieducational.com/inclusion.
Source: S. Fitzell, *Special Needs in the General Classroom: Strategies That Make It Work!* (Manchester, NH: Cogent Catalyst, 2007).

The Co-Teaching Book of Lists

List 8.18 Evaluation Process in a Co-Taught Classroom

Students

- Informal assessment information
- Formal assessment data
- Ongoing assessment
- Summative assessment
- Performance tasks and projects
  - Open ended
  - Complex
  - Authentic
- Observations
- Traditional quizzes
- Student interviews
- Analysis of student work
- Student-developed rubrics
- Student surveys
- Parent feedback

Parents

- Student study team input
- Parent conferences
- Parent surveys
- Home-school newsletter

Teachers

- Planning meetings
- Reflection sheets
- Daily feedback forms
- Co-teaching communication cards
- Observer feedback

List 8.19   Accommodations for Testing in a Co-Taught Classroom

- Many techniques can be used in a co-taught classroom to evaluate the learning and achievement of your diverse learners; some techniques may be more appropriate for certain kinds of learners
- Distinguish ongoing, authentic assessment processes from more formal and summative measures
- Assessment in a co-taught classroom needs to be flexible and adjusted to the needs of the learners
- Often students with mild to moderate learning disabilities are able to learn course material, but may have difficulty demonstrating what they know through traditional written tests that are summative
- Assessment of student learning involves finding alternative ways for students to demonstrate their mastery of the material
- Necessary modifications should be delineated in the student's IEP

Here are some strategies to ponder before, during, and after a test:

Before the Test

- Use of study note cards
- Concept maps
- Study guides
- Graphic organizers
- Practice quizzes
- Small-group and partner review
- Keyword method
- Vocabulary preview sheet
- Cubing, using Bloom's taxonomy (see Chapter Nine)
- Question card relay (see Chapter Nine)
- Jigsaw book (see Chapter Nine)
- Flip books (see Chapter Nine)
- Test-taking techniques
- Making flash cards for study
- Use of mnemonics to remember steps and facts
- Examples of successful quizzes and tests that show acceptable work

During the Test

- Provide ongoing feedback
- Allow test to be completed verbally on tape
- Use short-answer format
- Allow use of electronic devices like spellcheckers and/or calculators

The Co-Teaching Book of Lists

- Create a quiet testing environment free of distractions
- Vary test format: oral tests, take-home tests, multiple-choice tests
- Demonstrate solutions to problems before test begins
- Offer teacher assistance
- Provide a word bank of key terms for student to use while taking the test
- Have the student check or circle the correct answer instead of writing it in the blank
- Have a paraprofessional read the text to the student
- Offer an alternative site or use of study carrel
- Extended time
- Have the student work with a learning partner to answer questions
- Keep a list of helpful test-taking techniques on student's desk

After the Test

- Make corrections by teacher, by group, individually, and in pairs
- Use alternative grading procedures (see List 8.20)
- Offer an opportunity to retake exam
- Offer multiple grades: one for content, one for mechanics, and one for thought processes and rationale
- Offer partial credit
- Give extra-credit questions and only count a certain number toward grade

Helpful Websites for Assessment

- Quia. www.quia.com
- Fun Brain. www.funbrain.com
- Quiz Center. http://school.discovery.com/quizcenter.html
- QuizStar. http://quizstar.4teachers.org

Taken from *The Co-Teaching Book of Lists*, by Katherine Perez. Copyright © 2012 by John Wiley & Sons, Inc.

List 8.20   Revising Grading Procedures

Assessment is one important aspect of evaluating all students in a co-taught classroom, and the dilemma of assigning grades to students can be a complex issue. This needs to be a collaborative effort between the general educator and the special educator.

Some factors to consider include:

- Teachers need to use their best judgment about students' abilities and needs and core course requirements
- When grading procedures differ significantly for students with special needs compared to their general education peers, the procedures should be described in the student's IEP and agreed on by both teachers
- Consider using the credit–no credit option instead of using letter grades
- If a student does unsatisfactory work, teachers should outline the steps necessary for the student to pass the exam

Taken from *The Co-Teaching Book of Lists*, by Katherine Perez. Copyright © 2012 by John Wiley & Sons, Inc.

Chapter 9

Instructional Strategies for Different Types of Learners

List 9.1   Getting Started with Strategies That Make a Difference

Engaging strategies are vital to the successful co-taught classroom. An integral part of your planning process should include the teaching techniques and interventions you will use to make a difference for all of your students. Your choice of strategies will depend on the co-teaching model, the specific learning styles of the students, and the flexible grouping methods you use.

Where should you start in developing appropriate strategies for your students?

- First make a list of challenges and strengths of the students with special needs in your class—how will these affect the learning process?
- Begin with clear learning goals
- What essential skills do students need to have to achieve these objectives and be successful?
- Have a toolbox on hand to enhance any lesson in designing strategies and options for instruction (see List 8.7)
- Make a list of techniques you have used to promote inclusion in your classroom and put a star next to the most successful ones—which students might benefit from these?
- Consider using more visuals, manipulatives, taped books, advance organizers, and the like to extend learning
- What are some of the challenges in implementing these techniques? How can you overcome these obstacles to reinforce the instruction in your classroom?
- Reflect on and evaluate which strategies are working and which are not working; use this information to guide future planning

Taken from *The Co-Teaching Book of Lists*, by Katherine Perez. Copyright © 2012 by John Wiley & Sons, Inc.

The Co-Teaching Book of Lists

List 9.2   Engaging Strategies for Co-Teaching

Voting. Ask students opening questions about the lesson you are beginning. Elicit their opinions about what they deem most important or which one is their favorite. This helps set a purpose for the lesson and creates a "need to know" while students ponder the main ideas to be shared. They vote with thumbs up or by raising their hands prior to the lesson.

Stack-a-Cup. Write facts, events, or content on the outside of paper cups. Students work with learning partners and stack their cups in sequence or hierarchical order, after making predictions of the order. This can work in a history lesson with timelines or in a story with sequence of events.

Underexplain with Learning Partners. Introduce the content of the lesson briefly. Match students with learning partners to work together bringing in their background knowledge to learn the material. This process boosts the students' higher-level thinking skills and gets them involved and supporting each other.

Emergency Task Cards. When students finish their work early, have a file box of task cards ready to engage your learners with independent tasks to extend and enrich their learning and to develop their higher-level thinking skills.

Question and Quick-Write. Pose a question and ask all students to jot down their answer on a card. This can also be done in pairs or small groups. This activity is designed to promote active thinking about a topic or an issue before engaging in classroom discussion. Quick-writes not only activate prior knowledge but also can be used to summarize key points of a lesson. Students can save these quick-writes over the course of the unit to aid in their reflection and to summarize key learnings.

Learning Contracts. These are independent agreements designed to meet the individual needs of your students. More details about these can be found later in the chapter, in List 9.24.

"Whip Around." Using an open-ended sentence stem or question prompt, ask the students to take turns responding with a quick response. This practice helps increase the number of students involved in the discussion and is an active way for all of your students to respond.

Lottery Tickets. When you "catch a student being good"—following directions or assisting another student, for example—reward him or her spontaneously with a lottery prize ticket. Then put the tickets into a large bowl for a weekly drawing. Prizes can include bonus points, free time, or tokens for prizes.

***Jeopardy* Game Review.** Design a game board similar to the *Jeopardy* TV game show for review of major ideas of a unit or a lesson. The categories and questions can be written on sticky notes. Students then form teams to review the content.

Choral Reading. Provide students with important facts from lesson. Have students repeat the statements in unison, responding to your prompts. A variation of this technique is called "triple talk": students repeat the phrase three times in response to teacher. This process boosts comprehension and retention and is a great reinforcer for auditory learners.

Think-Tac-Toe (Choice Boards). Give students a choice of nine to twelve different activities to extend their learning, and provide an opportunity of differentiated products. The options are usually developed to focus on the multiple intelligences or various learning styles. Samples of this technique are described later in this chapter, in Lists 9.5 and 9.6.

Links to Learning. Provide students with colored strips of construction paper. On each strip they write down an idea that they learned or a fact about the topic under discussion. They work with learning partners to share and link their learning together by taping the ends of the strip together to form an interlocking link after it has been looped to another idea. The partners then work with teams and loop their ideas together. This classroom chain continues to grow, and the teacher displays it as a decorative touch in the classroom. This is also a handy tool for review.

Keyboard Curriculum. Duplicate a keyboard template and place it inside a file folder. This is a hands-on approach to practice spelling words by tapping on the keyboard template. This can also be used for practicing math facts and vocabulary words as well.

"Text-Talk" Summary. Duplicate cell phone templates on paper and have students summarize the lesson using "text-talk" abbreviations. Share with a learning partner.

Headline Summary. Have students take notes on the lesson or the chapter they have just read. Then challenge them to pretend that they are newspaper reporters and they can only use ten words to create a headline that summarizes their notes.

Storyboard. Have students record main facts of a chapter or events in a story by creating a storyboard that depicts the events or facts in pictures instead of words. This is a great strategy for the visual learner or for the student who is a second language learner.

Team Poster. Students record individual reactions to the reading or the lecture or lesson. They work as a team to create a group poster to mount on walls to reinforce the visual memory of the content. Class can take a gallery walk to review the key ideas of other teams.

Slogans. After students have read a chapter, participated in a unit of study, or listened to a lesson taught, they work with a learning partner to create a "slogan" to help capture the essence of the lesson. The students share these slogans and then write them on sentence strips to mount on the classroom wall for greater reinforcement.

Rhyme, Rhythm, Rap. Students review their notes from a lesson or remember the facts of the chapter or story and create a rhyme, a rhythm, or a rap that is fun to perform for others and will help them retain key facts.

Picture It! Students read a passage and instead of writing down the main idea, they quickly capture what they found interesting in a graphic image, symbol, or a quick sketch. They then share it with a learning partner or a small group.

Silent Movies. Show students a brief video clip related to the subject of the lesson or novel you are reading *with the sound turned off*. Students then transcribe the dialogue and/or narration and discuss what they predict is being said. Replay the clip again with the sound and have them discuss their predictions. This increases student engagement and develops higher-level thinking skills as well as oral language skills.

Taken from *The Co-Teaching Book of Lists*, by Katherine Perez. Copyright © 2012 by John Wiley & Sons, Inc.

Activities for Planning Lessons

Logical and Mathematical Activities

- Ask questions
- Use diagrams: Venn diagram, cause and effect, fishbone, and timeline
- Graphs or charts
- Logic puzzles
- Analyze situations
- Crossword puzzles and Sudoku puzzles
- Strategy games
- Problem-solving number games
- Mental math
- Solutions and deductions
- Scientific experiments
- Number games

Visual and Spatial Activities

- Draw
- Paint
- Create a sculpture
- Design
- Geoboards
- Graphic organizers
- Use of colors: color-coded assignments
- Arrange items in order
- Overheads
- Photo stories
- Storyboards
- Videos
- Colored markers and pencils

Musical and Rhythmic Activities

- Match feelings and facts to rhythm
- Choral reading
- Move to music
- Echo clapping

- Create musical and rhythmic mnemonics
- Convert text notes to a rhyme, rhythm, or a rap
- Turn a story into a song
- Rewrite lyrics of a song to summarize key points of a lesson
- Use musical learning games
- Have students use patterns in their learning
- Build in percussion sticks or "clappers" or finger-snapping to reinforce facts

Interpersonal Activities

- Do activities that foster working with others
- Debate issues
- Take a class survey on certain issues to discuss opinions and beliefs
- Provide opportunities to have students teach others
- Cooperative learning
- Lead discussion
- Role-play situations
- Brainstorming
- Tutors or learning partners
- Organize events for class
- Dramatic play
- Create a learning line-up, where students form two parallel lines and discuss responses to questions with their partners. Rotate the lines so that they have a new partner with each new question.[1] This technique is also known as a Tea Party strategy.

Naturalistic Activities

- Rock studies
- Classification
- Animal studies
- Create projects from nature
- Classify attributes
- Make connections
- Nature study
- Categorize things
- Compare and contrast
- Field trips to explore naturalist connections to learning
- Notice relationships in science
- Difference of meanings
- Provide observation time for them to analyze and chart their findings

Taken from *The Co-Teaching Book of Lists*, by Katherine Perez. Copyright © 2012 by John Wiley & Sons, Inc.

Bodily and Kinesthetic Activities

- Acting
- Movement games
- Manipulatives
- Charades
- Role play
- Body language and gestures to describe meaning
- Dancing
- Sports
- Act or pantomime using word theater (acting out spelling words)
- Exercises
- Skits
- Standing workstations
- "Hop" to the right answer
- Puppets
- Interview a classmate about a topic
- Building structures to reinforce concepts
- Incorporating movement
- Teach someone else a skill or lesson learned

Intrapersonal Activities

- Provide quiet think time for reflection and analysis
- Provide opportunities for independent work
- Observe and make notations
- Keep a diary of what they learn each day
- Create crossword puzzles or chronological timelines related to the lesson
- Frame their thoughts in a journal or scrapbook
- Personal goal setting: keeping a timeline of their own activities
- Share meaningful personal experiences related to lesson
- Plan own agenda
- Poetry
- Listening to tapes
- Create a monologue related to the lesson
- Guided visualization

Verbal and Linguistic Activities

- Dictated stories
- Jokes and riddles
- Word games
- Tongue twisters

- Speeches
- Storytelling
- Conducting a mock interview
- Word sorts
- Writing in different genres
- Learning logs
- Creating a class newsletter, magazine, or journal
- Initiating vocabulary banks
- Giving presentations and demonstrations of key ideas learned

List 9.4   Product Possibilities

Provide a variety of different ways to present knowledge by selecting differentiated products according to the student's learning styles. Sometimes these products can be teacher choice, and sometimes you can allow the students to choose; this will depend on the content of the lesson, the age and abilities of the students, and the goals and objectives of the learning experience.

Role playing	Magazine article	Choral reading
Word bank	Collage	Bumper sticker
Game board	Mobile	Maze
Charades	Scavenger hunt	Storyboard
Drama	Skit	Question fan
Newspaper ad	Illustrated story	Skit
Mural	Survey	Advice column
Invention	TV commercial	Book jacket
Animated movie	Painting	Myth
Quiz	Brain teaser	Scrapbook
Diorama	Recipe	Poem
Crossword puzzle	Panel discussion	Card game
Debate	Greeting card	Billboard
Letter	Song	Monologue
Commentary	Cartoon	Survey
Logic puzzle	Lesson	Parody
Timeline	Proverb	Experiment
Sculpture	Interview	Fairy tale
Comic	Puppet show	Chart
Limerick	Flip book	Model
Autobiography	Sales pitch or	Team poster
Pantomime	commercial	Newscast
Panel discussion	Banner	Editorial
Video game	Classified ad	Alphabox
Script	TV program	Fact file
Postcard	Visual art form	Key vocabulary
Map	Demonstration	Want ad
Promotional brochure	Motto or slogan	Script
Bulletin board	Diary	Parable
Jump rope rhyme	Menu	Nursery rhyme
Model	Video	Wordless book
Recipe	Scavenger hunt	Speech

Instructional Strategies for Different Types of Learners   **195**

List 9.5   Think-Tac-Toe Choice Menus of Activities

In developing a differentiated classroom, providing student choice is an important component to consider. In a co-teaching setting, more choices help motivate even the most reluctant learners. Because of choice, students feel more empowered in the classroom. Choice promotes student accountability and responsibility, because "one size does not fit all." Proper procedures and routines are important to teach students how to make appropriate choices that arise from their needs and interests. Students also need to be taught the learning outcomes and how to self-assess their attainment of these goals.

What Are Choice Menus?

- Choice menus take different forms, depending on the age and ability levels of the students in the co-taught classroom
- The pattern of a tic-tac-toe game is used to produce a variety of products
- The menu of activities is developed by the teachers to align with the content of the lesson and to provide different outcome products according to the learning styles and readiness levels of the students
- The activities selected for the choice menus are placed in a grid that resembles a tic-tac-toe board or a quadrant activity sheet
- The purpose is to extend or reinforce the learning of a concept
- Can also be used as an alternative form of assessment to assess student mastery in an engaging and unusual way

How to Create a Choice Menu

- The graphic design that the teachers select can include three to nine options, depending on the model of choice menu used
- Each row may have a single theme or explore the same idea or subject across several disciplines
- Students choose their menu options and record what they are planning to do
- Rubrics are a helpful way for the students to self-assess and for the teachers to review their progress

Why Choice Is Important

- Choice provides opportunities for success for all students
- Active student engagement is promoted though choice
- Students are challenged at their appropriate level, and their learning styles are validated by the various activities
- As a tool for differentiation, students' independence and responsibility in the classroom are reinforced
- The activities vary in content, process, and product and can be tailored to address different readiness levels, learning styles, and student interests

List 9.6   Think-Tac-Toe Activity Board

Name _____

Topic _____

List 9.7   Vocabulary Bingo

Directions: Select one activity per day to make bingo. Your bingo card is due on
_____.

Write a story using ten of your vocabulary words	Complete page _____ in your vocabulary workbook	Write your vocabulary words and circle all the vowels	Draw a picture to symbolize six of your vocabulary words
Work with a learning partner to say, hear, and coach each other on the words of the week	Design a crossword puzzle using your vocabulary words	Sort your words into categories and label the categories	Alphabetize the vocabulary words
Choose three words and describe how they are connected to you and your life	Write your vocabulary words three times each on the screen	Create a rap, song, or poem using your vocabulary words	Go on a word hunt and find eight of your vocabulary words in books; cite the page number and the source
Draw a picture and hide your words in the picture	Make a collage with six of your words using newspaper and magazine clippings	Act out a skit using five of your vocabulary words	Write the definitions of six of the vocabulary words that you don't know the meaning of

Taken from *The Co-Teaching Book of Lists*, by Katherine Perez. Copyright © 2012 by John Wiley & Sons, Inc.

The Co-Teaching Book of Lists

List 9.8   Book Report Activity Board

Choose three different ways to show what you know about the book that you just read that will give you "tic-tac-toe."

Pantomime a part of the story and have others guess	Create a game for others to play to learn about the main events of the book	Produce a puppet show that retells the story
Memorize a passage from the book and perform it for the class with background music	Come up with your own unique way to show what you know (and be sure to get the okay from your teacher first)	Pretend you are a reporter covering an event from the story and write a newspaper article about it
Write a letter to the author telling how you felt about the book and ask clarifying questions	Give a persuasive speech to promote the book to others in the class	Create a story map of the main events in the book

List 9.9   Cubing

Cubing is a motivating way to differentiate curriculum using choice and chance and allows the student to have at least six variations of a task to complete related to the content of the lesson. When students work with cubes, they apply information in new ways.

Further differentiation can occur if teachers color-code the cubes to correspond to various readiness levels, student interest, or student learning styles.

As an example, each face of the cube could have one of the following open-ended prompts so that the cube can be used for multiple lessons:

- Who?
- What?
- Where?
- Why?
- When?
- How?

For younger students, each of these questions can be placed on a cube that is easily made out of small child-sized milk carton with the top removed and all sides covered with construction paper.

- Students read a story with a learning partner and pause to roll the cube.
- Depending on which question lands on top, they answer the question based on the facts of the story; then another student gets to roll

Other open-ended prompts include:

- Connect
- Analyze
- Compare
- Explain
- Diagram
- Synthesize

Adaptations

- Design cubes based on student interest or learning styles
- Create cubes around the multiple intelligences
- Use verbs from Bloom's Taxonomy to create tasks for students to do

An accompanying worksheet can be prepared in advance to give the students more details about the expected outcomes. You can also use dice to create the same effect. The students roll the dice and for whatever number lands on top, there is a corresponding task to accomplish listed on the worksheet.

The Co-Teaching Book of Lists

List 9.10   Cubing in the Content Areas

Listed here are some cubing tasks that can be used with specific content areas to help get you started. Consult the list of Bloom's Taxonomy of Higher-Level Thinking Skills to get more ideas for appropriate verbs to use in your subject and lesson.

Social Studies and English

- Tell a story
- Diagram events
- Debate points of view
- Describe
- Pretend
- Question
- Analyze
- Write a song
- Make a comic strip
- Evaluate
- Illustrate
- Apply
- Argue
- Restate
- Imagine
- Construct

Science

- List
- Use a Venn diagram
- Write a rule
- Diagram
- Figure out
- Use a graphic organizer
- Contrast
- Evaluate
- Hypothesize
- Construct
- Forecast
- Investigate
- Define
- Locate
- Critique

Mathematics

- Graph
- List
- Rearrange
- Evaluate
- Classify
- Calculate
- Prove
- Write a word problem
- Investigate
- Estimate
- Factor
- Solve
- Add
- Subtract
- Change
- Reduce
- Order
- Show symbols

Arts

- Create a sculpture
- Compose a song
- Make a model
- Do a skit
- Imagine
- Present
- Create a poster
- Show
- Sing
- Construct
- Compose
- Build
- Rearrange
- Pantomime

List 9.11   "Let 'em Roll": Cubing Task Cards

Lesson Goal _____

Teachers _____

ORANGE CUBE ACTIVITIES

1.

2.

3.

4.

5.

6.

GREEN CUBE ACTIVITIES

1.

2.

3.

4.

5.

6.

Question Prompts

Knowledge Level

How do you explain _____?

When did _____ happen?

List the _____.

What is _____?

How did _____ do it?

Where is _____?

Who was _____?

What were the main _____?

Comprehension

What ideas demonstrate _____?

How would you restate _____?

What is the theme of _____?

Can you tell me more about _____?

What facts support this idea _____?

What is meant by _____?

Why is _____ happening?

Application

What would happen if _____?

How would you support this idea _____ from the text or lesson?

What would be your solution for _____?

How would you relate _____ to _____?

How would you sequence _____?

Why is _____ important?

How is _____ an example of _____?

Taken from *The Co-Teaching Book of Lists*, by Katherine Perez. Copyright © 2012 by John Wiley & Sons, Inc.

Analysis

What is the overall main idea of _____?

What conclusions can you make about _____?

How is _____ related to _____?

Why do you think _____ happened?

What conclusions can you make about _____?

How would you differentiate between _____?

What evidence do you have about _____?

How would you categorize _____?

How would you justify _____?

What reasons can you give for _____?

Synthesis

How would you verify _____?

Can you develop a hypothesis for _____?

How would you modify _____ to develop a different _____?

What would happen if _____ was true?

How could you change the outcome of _____?
Why _____?

What could be done to reduce _____?

What could be done to increase _____?

Evaluation

How would you evaluate _____?

In what ways would you prioritize _____?

Tell me how to justify _____.

Why did you choose _____?

What are the implications of _____?

How would you rationalize the outcome of _____?

In what ways is it better to _____ than _____?

Do you agree with the outcome of _____?
Why _____?

What decision would you make about _____?

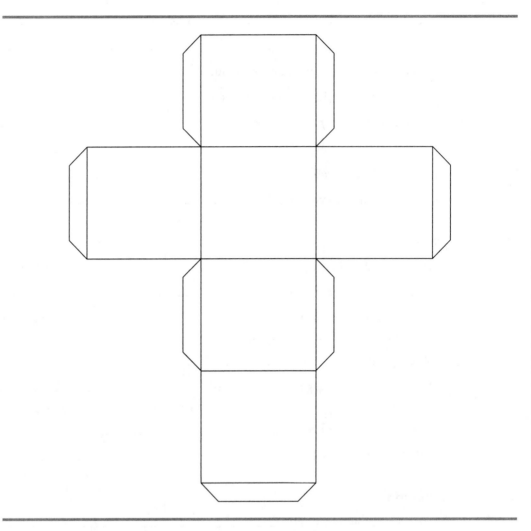

List 9.14   Cubing Companion Activity Sheet

Topic _____

Describe It	Compare It
Describe the main points of the lesson as you see it. How would you describe the issue or topic? Look at the subject closely and describe what you see using your senses	What would you compare this to? What are the similarities? What are the differences?
Associate It	**Analyze It**
What does this topic relate to? What does this subject make you think of? How does this topic connect to other subjects?	How would you break this subject into component parts? Tell how it is made. What does it consist of?
Apply It	**Argue for or Against It**
What are some ways that you can use these ideas? Tell what you can do with it. How does it help you understand other topics or issues?	Take a stand on this topic: argue for or against it. I am for this because _____. This works because _____. I agree(or disagree) because _____.

In the space below, write a paragraph about the topic based on your cubing answers. Add the responses of your team's ideas to the paragraph as well.

Verbs for Cubing and Questioning

Knowledge		Comprehension	
Retell	Name	Describe	Edit
Tell	Relate	Demonstrate	Locate
Memorize	Collect	Discuss	Find
Repeat	Label	Summarize	Report
Record	Restate	Recognize	Reword
List	Cite	Explain	Review
Recall	Recount	Express	Translate
Specify	Define	Restate	Identify
State	Know	Show	Paraphrase
Match	Identify	Indicate	Infer

Application		Analysis	
Inquire	Interpret	Experiment	Classify
Represent	Replicate	Distinguish	Arrange
Solve	Differentiate	Examine	Group
Indicate	Compare	Compare	Organize
Interview	Use	Survey	Differentiate
Question	Scrutinize	Scrutinize	Contrast
Simulate	Categorize	Categorize	Dissect
Imitate	Present	Probe	Diagram
Apply	Investigate	Investigate	Interpret
Display	Discover	Discover	Test
Employ	Contrast	Inquire	Analyze
Inspect	Detect	Find out	Plan
Collect	Produce	Correlate	Prioritize

Synthesis		Evaluation	
Assess	Evaluate	Pretend	Design
Correct	Determine	Create	Propose
Appraise	Decide	Invent	Incorporate
Revise	Resolve	Develop	Generalize
Rate	Score	Imagine	Originate
Propose	Choose	Hypothesize	Prepare
Recommend	Conclude	Assemble	Predict
Critique	Advise	Construct	Forecast
Estimate	Consider	Compose	Speculate
Amend	Judge	Devise	Theorize
Grade	Suggest	Plan	Systematize
Validate	Appraise	Formulate	Collaborate

Taken from *The Co-Teaching Book of Lists*, by Katherine Perez. Copyright © 2012 by John Wiley & Sons, Inc.

List 9.16   Graphic Organizers

Graphic organizers are powerful learning tools, especially for visual learners. They come in many shapes and sizes and can be used in multiple ways with any content area. Graphic organizers are visual recording strategies used to summarize and synthesize information learned.

As a visual representation, they provide a means for structuring and organizing information to show the interrelatedness of topics or for arranging the sequence of events in a topic. As a summary and synthesis tool, graphic organizers are important to use in reading, writing, note taking, and discussion. Many students with special needs think graphically instead of using a linear structure of a formal outline.

Following are some of the many different forms of graphic organizers:

- Venn diagrams
- Brainstorming charts
- KWL charts
- Story maps
- Double-entry journal
- Concept maps
- Five Ws chart
- Sequence chart
- Word webs
- Four-column charts
- Fishbone or herringbone charts
- Fact and opinion
- Cause-and-effect charts
- T charts
- Cyclical flow charts

List 9.17   Why Use Graphic Organizers?

Graphic organizers help a wide array of students classify ideas and communicate more effectively in a number of contexts. You can use graphic organizers to structure thoughts for writing, for problem solving, studying, reviewing, planning, and brainstorming. Listed here are some of their main benefits. Graphic organizers can:

- Assist students in retaining and transferring knowledge
- Incorporate varied forms of visual representation and charting
- Help students organize and process material being learned
- Provide a focus for small-group work
- Be used as tools for authentic assessment
- Help support independent study work for advanced learners
- Assist with curriculum planning and unit development
- Provide students with successful ways to organize, interpret, and synthesize information learned
- Help students retrieve prior knowledge
- Give students an opportunity to visualize what they are learning
- Engage students in gathering and supplying data
- Activate students' higher-level thinking skills
- Help students link information to what is known

List 9.18   How Do You Use Graphic Organizers?

- Determine the topic that you wish to explore with the students and which form of visual representation would work best
- Select the structure that will best record the necessary information
- Make the graphic organizers big and bold
- Model the use of graphic organizers with the overhead or on a chart
- Invite and engage students to gather and supply the needed data
- Engage students in gathering and supplying data to construct the organizers
- Model the process for the students by filling in the elements of the selected graphic organizers
- Evaluate the results for any missing information that students want to provide
- Have students work with learning partners or work in small groups
- Give students time to brainstorm ideas before writing them down on a chart
- Have students post their charts around the room and discuss highlights with group
- Give students time to walk around the room, review the charts of others, and jot down new ideas
- Discuss what they learned
- Give them another opportunity to add to their charts
- Model on the overhead first, then let the students create their own graphic organizers; avoid cookie-cutter approaches that make graphic organizers resemble just another worksheet to complete
- Provide struggling students with a list of categories to help them get started on their cluster or semantic maps
- Set clear criteria for the lesson so that students understand the objective and use of the graphic organizer

List 9.19   Herringbone Graphic Organizer

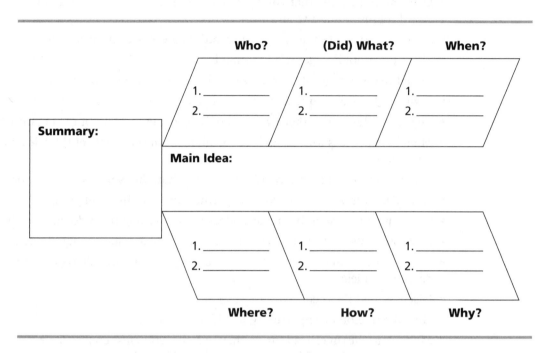

Some reading and language arts teachers have adapted the herringbone questions to reflect literary elements of the book or story.

1. Who?   The character(s)

2. What?   The action occurring

3. When?   The time

4. Where?   The setting or location

5. How?   The quality associated with the action

6. Why?   The motive or reason

7. Main idea   Major theme of the story or book presented

Taken from *The Co-Teaching Book of Lists*, by Katherine Perez. Copyright © 2012 by John Wiley & Sons, Inc.

List 9.20   Double-Entry Journal

Quote from Text or Story	My Thoughts, Reactions, and Connections

List 9.21   Learning Centers

While the teachers in a co-teaching classroom are working with small groups of students at stations or learning centers, the other students need to know how to use appropriate procedures and routines for working independently. Each center should focus on a different task or activity, with clearly defined outcomes; this assists in the process of differentiation and engages all learners.

Through the use of learning centers advanced learners are able to extend and enrich their learning, and struggling students have an opportunity to dig deeper into the content to broaden their understanding. Centers can be further differentiated by focusing in on different learning styles and multiple intelligences.

What?

- Centers need to be directly related to content, not just provide busywork for the students.
- Usually three to five centers can be managed in a co-taught classroom, with each teacher supporting one center and the other students working in small groups at the other centers
- Centers provide a collection of materials for further exploration set up around the classroom
- Provides an opportunity for one teacher to assess a small group of students while the other teacher oversees the use of the centers

How?

- Students should be flexibly grouped at centers, not grouped according to fixed ability
- Students can rotate among the centers according to a schedule, or the teacher can assign specific students to centers to develop certain skills
- Teachers should explain the purpose and process of each station before students move
- Directions should be clear and simple
- Select a facilitator for each group
- Tasks selected for the centers should be active and engaging and provide hands-on experiences for the students
- Teachers should move around the centers to monitor progress and time on task and assist and support as needed
- Students need to be accountable for what they learn and accomplish at the center; use a simple reflection sheet to be completed after center time

Why?

- Promotes independent learning on the part of the students
- Meets the needs of diverse learners
- Provides self-paced learning and builds responsibility
- Is an active and engaging way to reinforce the concepts in a lesson

Types of centers

- Listening center
- Math
- Technology
- Art
- Reading
- Vocabulary and spelling
- Puzzles
- Writing
- Science

Unit _____

Objectives _____

ACCOUNTABILITY

   1. How I worked:

   2. What I accomplished:

   3. What I learned:

List 9.23   Keeping Students on Target

Task Cards

- As students enter the room, they each receive a task card that provides expectations for tasks to be accomplished and due dates
- Some students may have a learning contract (to be discussed later in this chapter, in List 9.24)
- Task cards can be individualized or color-coded for small-group work
- Outcomes can be scaffolded for students who need extra reinforcement

Agendas

- Post a daily agenda so students know who will be doing what, with whom, and by when
- Daily agendas should be posted on the board for all to see
- When your differentiated program is more established, these agendas can be personal (for independent study), smaller interest groups, or for station activities in small groups

Depending on your co-teaching program, some students may need independent learning contracts to complete specified work that is tailored to their individual needs. In these cases, refer to the sample independent study contract in List 9.24.

Student name _____

I am interested in:

What I will be learning about:

I will need the following resources and materials:

This is what I will do:

This is how I will demonstrate what I learned:

I will present my product on:

Student Signature _____

Date _____

Teacher Signature _____

Date _____

Taken from *The Co-Teaching Book of Lists*, by Katherine Perez. Copyright © 2012 by John Wiley & Sons, Inc.

List 9.25   Anchor Activities

- Anchor activities should be an integral part of a co-teaching program to ensure greater student engagement
- Anchor activities provide students with choices if they finish their work early or complete their station activities
- Anchor activities can also be completed by one portion of the class while the teachers are instructing the rest of the class
- The activities should require no direct instruction time and should be completed independently
- These activities are intended to review or extend learning of the subject matter, not to be just busy work
- All tasks should be relevant to the concepts being developed in the class
- Provide an opportunity for students to do something that is less demanding and causes less stress

Following are some suggested anchor activities:

- Make-up work
- Independent choice reading
- Skill practice
- Word puzzles or crossword puzzles related to topic
- Word sorts
- Sentence sequencing
- "Problems of the Week"
- Math games
- Vocabulary flash cards
- Review game
- Web search options
- Assigned reading
- Quick-write activities
- Journal writing

List 9.26   Activating Strategies

Teachers can use activating strategies to activate students' prior knowledge, build background, set the stage for learning, and create a need to know:

1. KWL strategy: What I **K**now, What I **W**ant to learn, What I did **L**earn[2]
2. Quick writes
3. Anticipation guides
4. Brainstorming
5. Teacher read-alouds
6. Making predictions
7. Video clips
8. Text tour
9. Concept web
10. Clustering
11. Focus questions (Have you ever . . . ? What if . . . ?)
12. Posters
13. Discussion
14. Think-pair-share[3]
15. Guided imagery
16. Story
17. Role play
18. Agenda map
19. Synectics: how does this picture relate to what we will be learning?
20. Three-step interview: students take turns interviewing each other about the topic in teams of three

Taken from *The Co-Teaching Book of Lists*, by Katherine Perez. Copyright © 2012 by John Wiley & Sons, Inc.

The Co-Teaching Book of Lists

List 9.27   Techniques to Set the Stage for Learning

Anticipation Guide

- A prereading strategy usually done independently by the student
- Students make predictions about the text or topic to be learned, which stimulates comprehension
- Activates students' background knowledge, feelings, and opinions about a topic
- Promotes critical thinking and makes reading more enjoyable

Implementation

- Teacher identifies major concepts to be learned
- Teacher creates a series of statements
- Students read statements and decide if they agree or disagree with the statement
- Students make predictions and discuss their opinions
- Teacher assigns text to be read or delivers lesson
- At the end of the lesson, students revisit anticipation guide and may change responses using new knowledge gleaned from lesson
- Teacher discusses correct responses, and students support with citations from text

Visual Instruction Plan (VIP). Teacher designs a step-by-step visual graphic image of the directions for an assignment. This scaffolds the directions for students who need to see the progression of steps necessary for completion.

Sticky Note Discussion. Pose an open-ended question to the students regarding the topic to be studied. Give them adequate think time. They jot down their answer or idea on the sticky note with pictures, words, or phrases. After sharing with a learning partner, they place their sticky notes on the board or chart paper where the question was posed. As an activator, this is an excellent way to see at a glance the background knowledge that your students have. In this way, it is an excellent needs assessment tool. This strategy can also be used as a summarizer to reflect on what they know.

Mini-case Study Solution. Present a problem or a mini-case to the students before beginning the lesson. Have the class attempt to solve the case or dilemma without reading the text. This motivates the learners to read and find out the correct solution and compare results. This processes engages their curiosity and higher-level thinking skills.

Advance Organizers

- Outlines
- Mnemonic devices
- One-page summary
- Graphic organizers
- Preview questions; do a quick-write
- Vocabulary preview

Instructional Strategies for Different Types of Learners   **221**

Quote Card Match. This text previewing strategy is an active way to set a purpose for the lesson and to reduce the reading load for students who may struggle with reading. Teachers select six to eight significant quotes from the book or lesson and place them on index cards. These cards are distributed to students, who read their card and predict what the chapter or lesson will be about. They then mingle and share their quote with a learning partner. Together they make a new prediction. One more mix and then the class discusses their predictions. While reading the text, ask them to become ''word detectives'' and highlight the quote in the text or story.

Chart Chatter. Post charts around the room that list various topics related to the unit of study. Have students work in teams to activate prior knowledge by jotting down their ideas about the topic. Moving on to other charts, they add their ideas to those as well. This activity involves movement and is an excellent way to engage students on subject matter content. They can add to the charts after the lesson or unit is complete.

Word Sorts. This prereading activity is an excellent technique for students to share their background knowledge. Students work with a learning partner and are provided with a list of key vocabulary words. They cut them apart into word chips and categorize them, making predictions before the lesson begins They can do word sorts by word families, prefixes and suffixes, parts of speech, and so on.

Predict a Passage. Provide students with a list of key words from the chapter or story they are about to read. They work with a learning partner to sequence the key words in an order that tells a story or a sequence that predicts events in the chapter. They write their sentences or stories that contain these words and share them.

List 9.28   Strategies to Support Learning During Instruction

The strategies listed here will support students' learning and maintain engagement of the students during the lesson. Comprehension is no longer just something we do "after the lesson" to check for understanding. Rather, comprehension needs to be fostered throughout the learning process for greater retention.

- Paired reading
- Teacher read-alouds
- Graphic organizers
- Pause and share with a learning partner
- Simulation
- Role-plays
- Guided practice
- Double-entry journals
- Quick-writes
- Learning logs
- Reader's theater
- Dramatization
- Oral interpretation
- Story board
- Student-generated questions
- Small-group or whole-class discussion
- Personal response
- Compare and contrast (Venn diagram)
- Prediction or speculation
- Interpretation of key passages
- Paraphrase with a partner
- Character analysis

List 9.29   A Closer Look: During-Instruction Strategies

Highlight Vocabulary. Use highlighting tape that has been cut into small strips so that students can highlight words they are not sure of in the text as they read. These strips of highlighting tape can be reused again by placing the strips on an index card that has been laminated. After the reading, the student writes down the challenging words and looks for context clues. Working with a learning partner, the student attempts to define the words. The tape is then removed and placed back on the index card for further use.

VIP Strategy. Teacher decides how many VIPs (very important points) she or he wants the students to find in a specific reading selection or chapter and provides each student with one large sticky note that has been cut into three to four strips. The student then reads along and tags a VIP with a sticky note strip. The important points are then shared with a learning partner, and this results in a much richer class discussion.

Word Window. Cut a rectangular opening in the middle of an index card large enough to reveal six to eight words in a line. This "window" will help students highlight and frame portions of text to assist them with the decoding process and avoid unnecessary visual distractions. A variation on this technique is to cover the opening with colored plastic transparency material to enhance the contrast of the print. This simple modification can assist and support struggling readers.

Every-Pupil Response Techniques. Pause during the lesson to check in with the students. Using simple every-pupil response techniques not only keeps your students attentive and engaged, it also provides an excellent way to informally assess student understanding. Here are some ways to accomplish this:

- Thumbs up or thumbs down (do they understand the concept or not?)
- Students use individual whiteboards to record responses or use yes-or-no cards to respond
- Students give you a "fist of five," showing five fingers if they "get it" in a gradual scale down to one finger if they do not understand
- Students pair up with a learning partner, and each student has thirty to forty-five seconds to share what they found memorable in the lesson and then listen to their partner

Note Taking and Note Making. Students draw a line lengthwise down the middle of a sheet of paper to make two columns and record their notes on one side in a traditional format and do sketches of key ideas in the other column.

INSERT Coding Strategy. INSERT is an active during-reading activity developed by Vaughan and Estes.[4] This hands-on strategy is effective for less proficient readers because it provides them with opportunities to connect to text. Students use sticky notes to "tag" their texts and increase comprehension. The teacher and students decide on a set of codes for the class. Offered next are a few sample codes.

Coding System

1. X I disagree with this statement
2. + New and important information
3. ! Wow!

4. ? I don't understand this

5. * Very important to remember

How to Implement the INSERT Coding Strategy

1. Provide overview and purpose of the strategy and explain why it is helpful.

2. Model how to use it while doing a teacher read-aloud of text.

3. Guide the class by describing your thinking in using the codes.

4. Have students practice the technique with a learning partner and compare and discuss their codes.

5. Have students practice the technique independently.

6. Share coded ideas in a whole-class discussion.

List 9.30   After-Reading Strategies

The techniques listed here provide opportunities for students to reflect on their learning, connect their learning to new experiences, and boost comprehension and retention.

- Learning logs
- Text posters of key ideas
- Simulation
- Graphic organizers
- Role-plays
- Reporting out
- Culminating activity
- Revisit a KWL chart
- Revisit anticipation guide and agree or disagree
- Exit card (see full explanation in List 9.31)
- Reflective writing
- Critical review
- Research or I-search paper extending theme or topic
- Creative response to topic
- Rewrite the ending
- Debate or panel discussion
- Publication
- Newsletter
- Small-group or whole-class discussion
- Write a newspaper headline

The Co-Teaching Book of Lists

List 9.31   Summarizer Activities to Reflect on Learning

Concept Skits. Small groups of students work together to prepare a short skit that demonstrates the topic under study

Outcome Sentences. Have students reflect on the lesson and respond to the following open-ended prompts either in writing (exit card) or verbally (idea wave):
As a result of today's lesson:

- I learned...
- I now realize...
- I was surprised...
- I discovered...
- I observed...
- I am beginning to wonder...
- I am still curious about...
- I would like to find out more about...

Idea Wave. Use this verbal response technique after a lesson has been delivered. Students respond verbally, one at a time, about an idea they care to share. They can use one of the "outcome sentences" (shown in the preceding list) or share their own ideas. Here are some implementation ideas:

- Each student in the idea wave has a chance to share one idea
- The idea wave swirls around the entire class
- Each student responds or is given the option to pass
- Have students listen carefully to their peers' responses; if they have the same idea, they can either acknowledge the idea or think of a new and different idea

Exit Cards or Questions. This simple assessment technique can be used to check for understanding after a lesson. Provide each student with a card and a few minutes to complete whatever prompt you choose, depending on the age and ability levels of your students. This is a powerful strategy for students with special needs who might be hesitant to ask questions in class.

Meet them at the classroom door and explain that they need to submit their exit card to be dismissed for recess, to go home, or to change classes. You can easily scan the cards to see the main points of the lesson that they remembered and also to see any gaps in the learning to help you prepare tomorrow's lesson.

Have students sign their exit cards to increase accountability to help you any needed target intervention appropriately.

Teachers can create generic exit cards for students to complete at the end of class or use some sample exit questions and/or prompts for the cards:

- I understood today's lesson...
- Here are three main ideas from today:
- I was ready to learn today because...
- These are the questions that I still have:
- I can help others with...
- These are some strategies that I used to help me remember...
- I used my time wisely by...

- These are three new words I learned today:... Use these three new words in a sentence.
- These are the stations that I completed today:
- Three facts I learned today:
- Here is a definition of...
- Here is a prediction about...
- Here is an example of...
- This is the importance of...
- Make a headline about today's lesson.
- Where can you find more information on this?
- Write a question about...
- Give three facts that you remember. Why are these important?
- Use an analogy to compare what you learned with...
- Draw a picture of...
- What would happen if...?

Reflection Cards. These are variations on exit cards. Decide what you want the students to reflect and report on before leaving class that day. An example might be three important ideas, two new words I learned, and one question I still have. They can also list one question and one new idea.

Summary Swap. Pass out blank white sheets of paper to students. Have them write 1, 2, 3 in a row on their sheets. Then ask them to respond to prompts like these (which can be changed daily according to the lesson):

- Write down three key ideas you learned today.
- Write down three new words you learned today.
- Write down three things that were most important to you.
- Write down three successes you had today.
- Write down three questions for homework.

Four-Square Quick-Write. This instant graphic organizer gives students an opportunity to reflect and look deeper into the lesson of the day. Have them fold a sheet of paper into four quadrants. In each quadrant of the paper, they write a prompt (provided by the teacher) and their response to it. Sample prompts can include the following (and see Exit Cards, near the beginning of this list, for more ideas):

- Draw a symbol for...
- Why is _____ important?
- Write a question you have.
- Write three words to describe...
- Write three descriptors of the main character.

Literature or Historical Simulation. Have students play the parts of the characters they are studying or a scene from the period in history they are learning about. Have them act out scenes that are not in the book. Another option is to have them act out a scene from their own lives that relates to what they are studying.

Word Theater. Have small groups of students prepare and perform a brief skit that demonstrates the meaning of new vocabulary words learned in the lesson.

Taken from *The Co-Teaching Book of Lists*, by Katherine Perez. Copyright © 2012 by John Wiley & Sons, Inc.

The Co-Teaching Book of Lists

Picture Personification. Students create a tableau from a historical scene in the text and bring that scene to life, adding their own movements and dialogue. A variation on this strategy is to have the students select a character from the story, lesson, or text and write or speak a journal entry, letter, or article in the voice of that character. What would they say? What would they do?

Question Card Relay. Students are each given an envelope to write a question on. Inside the envelope there are three slips of paper or three blank index cards. Give the students time to think of a question about the story, lesson, or text you have recently studied. They write their question on the outside of the envelope and sign their name. Then students form groups of four to six. As in a relay, students pass their envelopes to the student to their right. That student reads the question and then gets a blank card out of the envelope to respond to. They answer the question to the best of their ability and sign the card. A signal is given and the envelope is once again passed. Each student receives a new envelope with a new question and finds a blank card to respond to. A signal is given for the final pass and the envelope is returned to the originator, who reviews the responses to his or her question. The teacher can then collect the envelopes and responses to use as an informal assessment of the questions students have and the accuracy of the answers students provide. Relays are swift, so teachers need to decide in advance how much time the students will have to respond. Depending on the age and ability level of the students, the time to respond can range from one to three minutes.

The Last Word. The topic to be summarized becomes an acronym. Students brainstorm all the things they can remember about the topic to create phrases that start with each of the letters of the topic. As a warm-up activity, have the students work on a "last word" summary about themselves.

List 9.32   Culminating Review Games

Some of your favorite sports and television game shows can be transformed to help students review what they have learned in an active, engaging, and motivating way. Here are some sample adaptations:

Who Wants to Be a Millionaire? Structure this activity like the game show and use student-generated questions and answers. Students or teachers develop questions related to the topic. Each question is presented in multiple-choice format. The questions become more difficult as you progress through the game. The payoff (in play money) also increases.

Password. Use for key vocabulary. Divide the class into partner teams who quiz each other by thinking of synonyms that describe the target word. Points are earned when students guess the "password," as on the television show.

Jeopardy. Use chart paper to draw a grid for the game. Place category headings across the top row, with descending dollar values in each column. Create four to six categories with five to six questions for each (students can create these questions). The first team calls out a category and dollar value, then answers. Monopoly money can be used as the cash prize. Whistles or other noisemakers can be used to signal a team's readiness to answer.

Baseball Review. Draw a baseball diamond on the overhead, on chart paper, or on the board. Divide the class into two teams. They take turns selecting questions that have been color-coded from easy to difficult. Students earn one base for the easiest and a home run for the most difficult. If a team misses a question, the other team has a chance to steal a base. For every question that is answered correctly, a base is earned and the marker is moved accordingly (a single, double, triple, or home run). Score is kept or a time limit is placed on game.

Hollywood Squares. There are two teams, and each team creates ten questions for the other team to answer. They draw a large tic-tac-toe square on the board or chart paper. The moderator calls out the question, and the corresponding team with the correct answer gets either an X or an O. You can cast nine class members as the "celebrities" who share their responses to the questions. The players decide who is right and respond.

Family Feud. Form two teams of students randomly. A question is posed to both teams. Students use desk bells or other noisemakers to respond. The first team to signal and respond correctly gets a point. Teams take turns until the review is complete.

Chapter 10

Reflecting on Practice and Planning Tools

List 10.1   Maintaining an Effective Co-Teaching Partnership

- Co-teaching is a relationship between two or more professionals
- Co-teachers progress through multiple stages in the development of their program
- Their progression in this process varies based on several factors:
  - Willingness
  - Skill level
  - Capacity
  - Prior relationship
  - Communication
- Understanding the developmental progression of co-teaching makes it possible to accept the realities and challenges of each phase
- Avoiding roadblocks and not getting stuck involves:
  - Recognizing difficulties
  - Empathy for partner
  - Realizing challenges
  - Open and honest communication
  - Patience
  - Structured time for planning
  - Time for reflection and goal setting

List 10.2   Taking It One Step at a Time

Stage 1: Beginning

Getting to Know You Stage

- May feel awkward at first
- Communication between teachers is superficial at first, with an emphasis on avoiding conflict
- General education teacher may have difficulty giving up the sense of ownership over the classroom and may feel a sense of intrusion or invasion
- Teachers develop a sense of boundaries
- Special educator may feel like an outsider and unhappy about giving up his or her own classroom; may feel unwelcome and detached
- Teachers attempt to develop from a social to a professional relationship
- Communication may be guarded, polite, and infrequent
- There may be a bit of a "my kids versus your kids" mentality

Stage 2: Negotiating

My Turn, Your Turn, Stage

- Co-teachers divide responsibilities
- More open and honest communication
- Sense of give-and-take communication
- Increase in professional communication
- Flexibility of roles increases
- Students see both as teachers, but often one remains the "main" teacher
- Struggling students tend to work with special educator
- Advanced learners tend to work with general education teacher
- Trust and collaboration increase

Stage 3: Mutual Respect

We're-Thinking-as-One Stage

- More open communication and interaction
- Both teachers have increased comfort level and acceptance
- Increased teacher confidence and competence
- Teachers complement each other in sharing the teaching

- Difficult to tell who is the "main teacher"
- Process becomes more "our class" and "our students"

Planning for the Future

- What are our strengths?
- Areas for improvement?
- Our collaborative goals:
  - What?
  - When?
  - How?
  - Who?
  - Outcomes?
- Next steps; action plan

Taken from *The Co-Teaching Book of Lists*, by Katherine Perez. Copyright © 2012 by John Wiley & Sons, Inc.

List 10.3   Co-Instruction: Where Are You Now?

Think of a person with whom you are currently co-teaching. Read through the preceding three phases of co-instruction. Place a checkmark beside items that represent the way you most frequently function as a co-teaching team. Then place a star (*) beside the next steps you would like to take toward co-instruction in the table here.

	Roles and Responsibilities	
	General Education Teacher	**Resource Staff (ESOL, Special Education, Reading, Title I, IA)**
Phase 1	_____ Writes lesson plans _____ Conduct instruction _____ Informs resource teacher of upcoming lesson _____ Periodically meets with resource teacher	_____ Modifies classroom materials as needed _____ Monitors instruction given to students with special learning needs by general education teacher _____ Implements behavioral interventions _____ Modifies and grades tests _____ Interacts primarily with students with special learning needs _____ Develops separate lesson plans and maintains a separate grade book _____ Periodically meets with general education teacher
Phase 2	_____ Writes lesson plans and shares with resource teacher _____ Shares formal instruction (presentation of a lesson) with resource teacher a minimum of once a week _____ Shares informal instruction (guided practice activities) for all students on a daily basis	_____ Plans with general education teacher on a weekly basis _____ Maintains a copy of general education teacher's lesson plans _____ Reviews tests with general education teacher in order to design modifications _____ Constructs classroom visuals (such as transparencies, written outlines, and study guides) _____ Assists with classroom management _____ Conducts formal instruction a minimum of once a week

(continued)

Reflecting on Practice and Planning Tools   **235**

	Roles and Responsibilities	
	General Education Teacher	**Resource Staff (ESOL, Special Education, Reading, Title I, IA)**
		_____ Provides regular informal instruction for all students on a daily basis _____ Develops and implements supplementary and supportive learning activities
Phase 3	_____ General education and resource teachers jointly plan and deliver instruction, with responsibilities shifting between the teachers _____ Both teachers monitor and assess all students in the class _____ Shared ownership of classroom duties is assumed _____ Planning is done on a daily basis to ensure classroom coordination _____ Lesson plans are jointly developed	

Source: Adapted from Stetson and Associates (www.stetsonassociates.com).

List 10.4   The Co-Teaching Rating Scale

Respond to each question below by circling the number that best describes your viewpoint. If you are not in a co-teaching relationship, rate the degree to which you feel each practice is important.

1. Rarely
2. Sometimes
3. Usually

1. I can easily read the nonverbal cues of my co-teaching partner.	1	2	3
2. I feel comfortable moving freely about the space in the co-taught classroom.	1	2	3
3. I understand the curriculum standards with respect to the content area in the co-taught classroom.	1	2	3
4. Both teachers in the co-taught classroom agree on the learning goals of the co-taught classroom.	1	2	3
5. Planning can be spontaneous, with changes occurring during the instructional lesson.	1	2	3
6. I often present lessons in the co-taught classroom.	1	2	3
7. Classroom rules and routines have been jointly developed.	1	2	3
8. Many measures are used for grading students.	1	2	3
9. Humor is often used in the classroom.	1	2	3
10. All materials are shared in the classroom.	1	2	3
11. I am familiar with the methods and materials with respect to this content area.	1	2	3
12. Modifications of goals for students with special needs are incorporated into this class.	1	2	3

13. Planning for classes is the shared responsibility of both teachers.	1	2	3
14. The "chalk" passes freely between two teachers.	1	2	3
15. A variety of classroom management techniques are utilized to enhance learning of all students.	1	2	3
16. Test modifications are commonplace.	1	2	3
17. Communication is open and honest.	1	2	3
18. There is fluid positioning of teachers in the classroom.	1	2	3
19. I feel confident in my knowledge of the curriculum content.	1	2	3
20. Student-centered objectives are incorporated into the classroom curriculum.	1	2	3
21. Time is allotted (or found) for common planning.	1	2	3
22. Students accept both teachers as equal partners in the learning process.	1	2	3
23. Behavior management is the shared responsibility of both teachers.	1	2	3
24. Goals and objectives in IEPs are considered as part of the grading for students with special needs.	1	2	3

Source: S. Gately and F. Gately, "Understanding Co-Teaching Components," *Teaching Exceptional Children* 33, no. 4 (2001): 40–7. The Co-Teaching Rating Scale.

The Co-Teaching Book of Lists

Name_____

Date_____

Step 1. Enter the values for each of the question numbers below. Then total each column.

Interpersonal Communication	Physical Arrangement	Familiarity with Curriculum
1.	2.	3.
9.	10.	11.
17.	18.	19.
Total _____	Total _____	Total _____

Curriculum Goals or Modification	Instructional Planning	Instructional Presentation
4.	5.	6.
12.	13.	14.
20.	21.	22.
Total _____	Total _____	Total _____

Classroom Management	Assessment
7.	8.
15.	16.
23.	24.
Total _____	Total _____

Reflecting on Practice and Planning Tools

239

Step 2. Plot the totals for each component on this Co-Teaching Rating Scale Profile.

	4	5	6	7	8	9
Interpersonal Communication						
Physical Arrangement						
Familiarity with Curriculum						
Curriculum Goals or Modification						
Instructional Planning						
Instructional Presentation						
Classroom Management Assessment						

List 10.5   Co-Teaching Road Map

What will we do?	What do we need?	When will we do it?

List 10.6   Looking Ahead: Planning Guide

List specific strategies or activities that you and your teaming partner will follow through on in your program.

What needs to be accomplished?	What steps are necessary to accomplish the task?	When will each step be done?	Who will do it?
A.	1. 2. 3.	1. 2. 3.	1. 2. 3.
B.	1. 2. 3.	1. 2. 3.	1. 2. 3.
C.	1. 2. 3.	1. 2. 3.	1. 2. 3.

Taken from *The Co-Teaching Book of Lists*, by Katherine Perez. Copyright © 2012 by John Wiley & Sons, Inc.

List 10.7   Student Profile

Name _____

Grade _____

Classroom Teacher _____

Subject _____

Special Educator _____

Paraprofessional _____

Areas of Student Strengths

Learning Preferences

Accommodations or Modifications

Behavior Management Strategies

Accommodations or Modifications for Grading and Assessment

List 10.8   Making the Most of Lesson-Planning Time

- Collaborate to develop an instructional routine you can agree on, and then create a lesson plan format that fits that routine
- Always come prepared to plan, and gather needed materials before the meeting
- When planning a unit, focus on the big ideas and outcomes; decide on the standards, content, assessments, products, and timeline; and plan for differentiation including learning activities, grouping, and adaptations
- If time is short, rotate the duties of deciding on lesson focus and making materials to support it
- You may find it easier for one teacher to plan the content and the other teacher to prepare the adaptations
- Plan a minimum of a week at a time; but when planning units, the scope and timeline will be broader

List 10.9   Co-Planning Agenda Framework

Step 1: Reflect on Previous Week

- Where are the students in relation to the goals established for last week?
- What worked well?
- What should we change?
- What can we learn from these needed changes?
- What about the students who didn't get it? How should we reteach concepts?
- How can we get better results?

Step 2: Develop a Learning Plan for Next Week

- Curriculum focus and content
- Evaluation and grading
- Learning strategies and activities
- Differentiation techniques
- Pacing of instruction
- Flexible grouping patterns
- What responsibilities will each of us have?
- Which co-teaching model would work best?

Step 3: Adjust Instruction to Fit Student Needs

- Which students need intensified instruction?
  - Individualized instruction
  - Peer tutoring
  - Cooperative group work
  - Modified materials
  - Adapted assignments
  - Testing accommodations
- Which students need curriculum expanded to keep them engaged?
  - How to maximize learning opportunities
  - How to extend learning in new directions

Step 4: Determine Resources Needed and Assign Responsibilities

- What materials will be needed?
- Which activities will each of us be responsible for preparing and teaching?

Taken from *The Co-Teaching Book of Lists*, by Katherine Perez. Copyright © 2012 by John Wiley & Sons, Inc.

List 10.10   Lesson Preparation Pointers

- After giving directions, have students restate the instructions with a learning partner
- For greater lesson mastery, show examples of successful completed assignments to give students a clear idea of your expectations
- Vary the kind of lessons presented and the format used to engage all learners
- Regularly change the output of information (your delivery) as well as the input of information (what you are requiring the students to do) to maintain attention to content
- Use the "I do, you do, we do" method of modeling and scaffolding instruction to guide students toward greater independence
- Allow for "brain breaks" in work time: after about ten minutes of content, give students a minute or two to process what they learned, changing the output of information given or the input required
- Encourage active, two-way discussions—if students are reticent to talk in the large group, have them share their ideas with a learning partner
- Reinforce learning with visual aids (such as graphic organizers, diagrams, and charts)
- Avoid giving multiple directions at one time; take it one step at a time
- Set the stage for learning when introducing a new topic by reviewing prior knowledge at the beginning of the lesson
- Teach students how to set their own goals; keep expectations realistic

List 10.11   Co-Teaching Lesson Planning Worksheet

Teachers involved _____

Date or period _____

Lesson objective(s)	
Standards(s)	

Lesson content _____

Process _____

Modifications

Special Education

Student	Target outcome	Modifications	Strategies	Evaluation

Co-Teaching Plan of Action

Co-Teaching Model	Grouping Needed	Outcome
What will be done?	By whom?	By when and how will it be measured?

Notes:

The Co-Teaching Book of Lists

List 10.12   Co-Teaching Lesson Planning Template

Topic Date Teachers	
Outcome(s)	
Content of lesson	Process
Evaluation of outcomes	Process
Data gathering (for needs assessment)	
Into, through, and beyond strategies	
Modifications needed	
Roles of co-teachers	

Notes:

List 10.13   Keeping Track

Focus students _____

Day	Objectives	Process	Evaluation	Roles of Teachers	Modifications	Product	Notes
Mon							
Tues							
Wed							
Thurs							
Fri							

Questions
for Discussion

Chapter 1: Co-Teaching in a Nutshell

1. What are some co-teaching indicators to look for in a classroom?

2. How would you define co-teaching in your own words?

3. What are some practices to avoid in a co-teaching situation?

4. What are some factors to consider in implementing a co-teaching program?

5. What are the major benefits of a co-teaching program for teachers? What are the major benefits for students?

6. Review the assumptions in List 1.14. Which ones resonate with you? Which assumptions are most important and why?

7. Complete the Anticipation Guide in List 1.15. Share with a learning partner your responses and opinions. Revisit the Anticipation Guide after completing your review of this book. Have any of your responses changed as a result of the knowledge you gained? Revisit the Anticipation Guide three months after you have implemented co-teaching. Have any of your opinions changed? Why?

Chapter 2: Co-Teaching Models

1. Where would you begin in selecting a co-teaching approach? What factors are most important to consider and why?

2. Does this chapter make you think differently about selecting an approach to co-teaching? How?

3. What are some strategies you would use to insure greater parity in the roles of the two teachers in a co-taught classroom?

4. Complete the activity in List 2.15 on applying the models. Discuss your results with a learning partner. What were some of the indicators that influenced your choices?

Chapter 3: Where Do You Start?

1. Create your own checklist for co-teaching using the steps and strategies described in this chapter. Where would you begin? How would you proceed?

2. Which factors do you consider most important in the planning process? Why?

3. How would you design your planning process and schedule your planning time? Which tools would you use?

4. Which teaching issues are most important to discuss with your partner?

5. Compare your results from List 3.15, Determining Roles and Responsibilities, with your teaching partner's results. Are you in agreement? If not, what are some considerations to ponder?

Chapter 4: Where Do You Go? A Co-Teaching Roadmap

1. How will you begin the scheduling process at your school? What are the steps that you will take?

2. What are the essential outcomes of your planning time with your co-teacher?

3. What procedures and routines do you have in place now in your classroom that would be helpful to share in a co-teaching situation? Which procedures do you want to improve on?

4. Which considerations and factors are most important to you in scheduling students for co-teaching?

5. What are some time management tips that you have found successful in managing your preparation and planning time for class? How would you share these with your co-teaching partner?

6. Name one strategy from this chapter that you plan to use in your classroom, and describe how you will implement it.

Chapter 5: Collaboration—Working as a Team

1. Think of all the teams to which you currently belong. Describe each team with one adjective, quality, or characteristic. Share your responses with a partner. What do these teams have in common?

2. What makes a team effective? Not effective?

3. Use List 5.3, Forming an Effective Co-Teaching Team, to discuss the most important issues for you in team formation.

4. Do you agree with the elements given in List 5.5, Relationship Building Blocks? What would you add to this list in light of your own experience?

5. Take time to reflect on and complete List 5.6, Team Preparation. Share your responses with a colleague. What did you learn about yourself? Why are these responses important in establishing a co-teaching partnership?

6. Read List 5.7, Personality Preferences. How can you work more effectively with different personality types?

7. What are the biggest challenges and roadblocks you expect to encounter in a co-teaching situation? How can you overcome these?

Chapter 6: Organizing and Planning for Success

1. Did this chapter make you think differently about how you organize your classroom to be more inclusive? Why or why not? What are some specific suggestions that you want to try?

2. How can you maximize the space in your classroom to be conducive for diverse learners?

3. Will you begin using flexible grouping in your classroom? Why or why not? How will you determine grouping patterns?

Taken from *The Co-Teaching Book of Lists*, by Katherine Perez. Copyright © 2012 by John Wiley & Sons, Inc.

4. What did you think about the suggestions for small-group success? Which strategies would be easiest for you to implement in your setting?

5. Describe topics or situations that would be best delivered in a large-class setting. Why? How would you do it?

6. What are some ways you might get your students ready to work independently? How would you monitor their success and outcomes?

7. What are the most important and successful procedures and routines that you have developed for your classroom? What strategies do you want to try next to foster a co-teaching environment?

8. Describe your classroom management philosophy. Would you need to modify this approach for co-teaching? Why or why not?

9. What assessments or methods do you use to learn about your students? Have you been satisfied with the results? What do you think about the suggestions provided in this chapter? Will they change your approach?

Chapter 7: Schoolwide Organization—Administrative Issues

1. Did this chapter make you think differently about implementing co-teaching at your school site? In what ways?

2. What is your current plan for inclusion?

3. What are the challenges your school and staff are facing with the co-teaching process? Which strategies in this chapter will help you overcome these?

4. What is your action plan and timeline for moving forward with co-teaching? Where will you start? What are your desired outcomes?

5. How will you determine whether you are successful?

6. Who will be involved in scheduling and placement issues? What ideas did you gain from this book to assist you in this process?

7. How does a student study team support co-teaching and collaborative decision making?

8. In what ways will you support the teachers in the co-teaching process? The students? How will you involve the parents in this process?

9. What systems are in place for evaluating the effectiveness of co-teaching? What tools from the book will you use?

10. How will observation, feedback, and coaching be fostered among the teachers involved in co-teaching?

Chapter 8: Accommodations and Modifications That Make a Difference

1. How can you meet individual needs in your classroom and still maintain high standards?

2. How can both teachers contribute to modifying the curriculum and accommodating for different needs?

3. What strategies are most important to you in implementing your co-teaching program?

4. At what point do we stop making modifications and adaptations and expect students to make it on their own?

5. Did this chapter make you think differently about modifying instruction for students with special needs? In what ways?

6. How will you begin accommodating and adapting instruction?

7. Discuss your responses to List 8.11, Adaptation Application Activity, with a partner. What were the indicators that helped you choose? Did you agree or disagree?

8. What instructional supports do you find most helpful in your co-teaching program?

9. Describe a challenging student in your class to a learning partner. What successful adaptations have you tried? Which adaptations did not work? Share strategies for success.

10. How would you use List 8.16, Adaptations and Modifications Chart, in your co-teaching classroom?

Chapter 9: Instructional Strategies for Different Types of Learners

1. What are some of the techniques you use to engage your students?

2. Review the strategies in List 9.2, Engaging Strategies for Co-Teaching. Which ones do you plan to use in your classroom, and how will you implement them?

3. Think about your own learning style. In considering the multiple intelligences, what are your own strengths? How do these affect your teaching style?

4. Working with a partner, choose a topic or content area. What are some ways that you could design a multiple intelligence lesson to teach this?

5. What are some of the ways that you learn about the strengths of your students? How does this affect your instruction?

6. What role does student choice play in a co-teaching classroom?

7. Consider a topic that you will soon be teaching. Review the product possibilities in List 9.4. How many of these would be appropriate for the lesson?

8. Working with a partner, design a Think-Tac-Toe board together. Refer to Lists 9.5 and 9.6 to get you started.

9. What would you like to learn more about to differentiate the content, process, or products of your lessons?

Chapter 10: Reflecting on Practice and Planning—Tools for Moving Ahead

1. Where are you in the developmental process of co-teaching? Refer to the phases described in List 10.2, Taking It One Step at a Time.

2. Complete the survey in List 10.3, Co-Instruction: Where Are You Now? Share your responses with your co-teaching partner. What are your next steps?

Appendix

3. In reflecting on the co-teaching process, what is most important to you? Complete List 10.4, The Co-Teaching Rating Scale. Plot your totals for each component. Engage in a small-group discussion of your results.

4. Based on your reflections from the previous surveys, work with your co-teaching partner on drafting a road map in List 10.5.

5. You are now ready to fine-tune your future plans. Complete List 10.6, Looking Ahead: Planning Guide.

6. What do you want to learn more about, now that you have read this book?

Notes

Introduction

1. T. Bennett, D. Deluca, and D. Burns, "Putting Inclusion into Practice: Perspective of Teachers and Parents," *Exceptional Children* 64, no. 1 (1997, Fall): 115–31; P. J. Rea, V. L. McLaughlin, and C. Walther-Thomas, "Outcomes for Students with Learning Disabilities in Inclusive and Pullout Programs," *Exceptional Children* 68, no. 2 (2002): 203–22.
2. A. Ford, K. Davern, and R. Schnorr, "Learning with Significant Disabilities: Curricular Relevance in an Era of Standards-Based Reform," *Remedial and Special Education* 22, no. 4 (2001): 214–22.

Chapter One

1. L. Adams and K. Cessna, "Metaphors of the Co-Taught Classroom," *Preventing School Failure* 37 (1993): 28–31.
2. L. Cross and D. Walker-Knight, "Inclusion: Developing Collaborative and Cooperative School Communities," *Educational Forum* 61, no. 3 (1997): 269–77; C. Hughes and W. Murawski, "Lessons from Another Field: Applying Co-Teaching Strategies to Gifted Education," *Gifted Child Quarterly* 45, no. 4 (2001): 196–204.
3. C. S. Walther-Thomas, "Co-Teaching Experiences: The Benefits and Problems That Teachers and Principals Report over Time," *Journal of Learning Disabilities* 30 (1997): 395–407.
4. Adams and Cessna, "Metaphors of the Co-Taught Classroom."
5. N. Zigmond, K. Magiera, and D. Matta, "Co-Teaching in Secondary Schools: Is the Instructional Experience Enhanced for Students with Disabilities?" Paper presented at the annual Council for Exceptional Children conference, Seattle, WA, 2003.
6. M. Friend and L. Cook, *Interactions: Collaboration Skills for School Professionals,* 4th ed. (Boston: Allyn & Bacon, 2003); S. Saland, M. Johansen, J. Mumper, A. Chase, K. Pike, and J. Dorney, "Cooperative Teaching: The Voices of Two Teachers," *Remedial and Special Education* 18, no. 1 (1997): 3–11.
7. Cross and Walker-Knight, "Inclusion."
8. P. Hunt, M. Alwell, F. Farron-Davis, and L. Goetz, "Creating Socially Supportive Environments for Fully Included Students Who Experience Multiple Disabilities," *Journal of the Association for Persons with Severe Handicaps* 21, no. 2 (1996): 53–71.

9. L. Dieker, *The Co-Teaching Lesson Plan Book: Academic Year Version*. (Whitefish Bay, WI: Knowledge by Design, 2002).

10. Zigmond, Magiera, and Matta, "Co-Teaching in Secondary Schools."

11. D. Boudah, J. Schumaker, and D. Deschler, "Collaborative Instruction: Is It an Effective Option for Inclusion in Secondary Classroom?" *Learning Disability Quarterly* 20, no. 4 (1997): 293–315.

12. Walther-Thomas, "Co-Teaching Experiences."

13. J. Bauwens and J. Hourcade, "Cooperative Teaching: Pictures of Possibilities," *Intervention in School and Clinic* 33, no. 2 (1997): 81–5, 89; L. Cook and M. Friend, "Co-Teaching: Guidelines for Creating Effective Practices," *Focus on Exceptional Children* 28, no. 2 (1995): 1–12.

14. L. Dieker, "Rationale for Co-Teaching," *Social Studies Review* 37, no. 2 (1998): 62–5.

15. U.S. Department of Education, *Glossary of Terms* (July 2004). Retrieved April 20, 2008, from http://http://www2.ed.gov/nclb/index/az/glossary.html.

16. Least Restrictive Environment Coalition. Retrieved April 20, 2008, from http://http://www.lrecoalition.org.

Chapter Two

1. M. Friend, *Co-Teach! A Handbook for Creating and Sustaining Successful Classroom Partnerships in Inclusive Schools* (Greensboro, NC: MFI, 2008).

Chapter Nine

1. S. Kagan, *Kagan Cooperative Learning* (San Clemente, CA: Kagan Publishing and Professional Development, 1994).

2. D. M. Ogle, "K-W-L: A Teaching Model That Develops Active Reading of Expository Text," *Reading Teacher* 39 (1986): 564–70.

3. Kagan, *Kagan Cooperative Learning*.

4. J. Vaughn and T. Estes, *Reading and Reasoning Beyond the Primary Grades* (Needham Heights, MA: Allyn & Bacon, 1986).

Additional Resources

Adams, L., Cessna, K., and Friend, M. *Colorado Assessment of Co-Teaching (CO-ACT)*. Denver: Colorado Department of Education, 1993.

Armstrong, T. *In Their Own Way: Discovering and Encouraging Your Child's Multiple Intelligences*. New York: Tarcher/Putnam, 2000.

Armstrong, T. *Multiple Intelligences in the Classroom*. Alexandria, VA: ASCD, 2000.

Austin, V. L., "Teachers' Beliefs about Co-Teaching," *Remedial and Special Education* 22 (2001): 245–55.

Bauwens, J., Hourcade, J. J., and Friend, M. "Cooperative Teaching: A Model for General and Special Education Integration." *Remedial and Special Education* 10, no. 2 (1989): 17–22.

Beninghof, A. *Ideas for Inclusion: The Classroom Teacher's Guide to Integrating Students with Disabilities*. Longmont, CO: Sopris West, 1997.

Beninghof, A. M. *Making Inclusion More Successful* (videos and staff development guides). Belleview, WA: Bureau of Education and Research, 2000.

Beninghof, A. M. *Engage All Students Through Differentiation*. Peterborough, NH: Crystal Springs, 2006.

Chapman, C., and King, R. *Differentiated Assessment Strategies*. Thousand Oaks, CA: Corwin Press, 2005.

"Cubing: A Perspective Writing Exercise." *Teaching Today,* July 18, 2007. Retrieved Feb. 16, 2012, from http://teachingtoday.glencoe.com/downloads/topic/writing-skills.

DeBoer, A. *Working Together: The Art of Consulting and Communicating*. Longmont, CO: Sopris West, 1995.

DeBoer, A. *Working Together: Tools for Collaborative Teaching*. Longmont, CO: Sopris West, 1995.

Deschenes, C., Ebeling, D. G., and Sprague, J. *Adapting Curriculum and Instruction in Inclusive Classrooms: A Teacher's Desk Reference*. Bloomington, IN: Indiana University, 1994.

Deshler, D. D., Palincsar, A. S., Biancarosa, G., and Nair, M. *Informed Choices for Struggling Adolescent Readers: A Research-Based Guide to Instructional Programs and Practices*. Newark, DE: International Reading Association, 2007.

Dieker, L. "What Are the Characteristics of 'Effective' Middle and High School Co-Taught Teams?" *Preventing School Failure* 46, no. 1 (2001): 14–25.

Dover, W. *The Personal Planner and Training Guide for the Paraprofessional*. Manhattan, KS: Master Teacher, 1996.

Fairfax County Public Schools. *Primary Purposes: Language Arts Resource Guide*. Fairfax, VA: Instructional Services Department, 1995.

Fairfax County Public Schools. *Expanding Expectations: Language Arts Resource Guide*. Fairfax, VA: Instructional Services Department, 1996.

Fennick, E. "Co-Teaching: An Inclusive Curriculum for Transition." *Teaching Exceptional Children* 33, no. 6 (2001): 60–6.

Fitzell, S. *Special Needs in the General Classroom: Strategies That Make It Work!* Manchester, NH: Cogent Catalyst, 2007.

Ford, M., and Opitz, M. "Using Centers to Engage Children During Guided Reading Time." *The Reading Teacher* 55, no. 8 (2002): 710–13.

Friend, M. *Successful Co-Teaching Strategies: Increasing the Effectiveness of Your Inclusive Program (Grades 1–12)*. Bellevue, WA: Bureau of Education and Research, 2004.

Friend, M. *The Power of Two: Making a Difference Through Co-Teaching* (video). Port Chester, NY: National Professional Resources, 2005.

Friend, M. *Co-Teach! A Handbook for Creating and Sustaining Successful Classroom Partnership in Inclusive Schools*. Greensboro, NC: MFI, 2008.

Friend, M., and Bursuck, W. *Including Students with Special Needs: A Practical Guide for Classroom Teachers*. 5th ed. Boston: Allyn & Bacon, 2009.

Friend, M., and Cook, L. *Interactions: Collaboration Skills for School Professionals*. 5th ed. Boston: Allyn & Bacon, 2007.

Gable, R. A., Hendrickson, J. M., Evans, S. S., Frye, B., and Bryant, K. "Cooperative Planning for Regular Classroom Instruction of Students with Disabilities." *Preventing School Failure* 37, no. 4 (1993): 16–20.

Gardner, H. *Multiple Intelligences*. New York: Basic Books, 2006.

Hamlin, M. *Inspiring Active Learning: A Handbook for Teachers*. Alexandria, VA: ASCD, 1994.

Hammeken, P. *Inclusion: An Essential Guide for the Paraprofessional*. Thousand Oaks, CA: Corwin Press, 2003.

Janney, R., and Snell, M. E. *Modifying Schoolwork*. Baltimore: Paul H. Brookes, 2000.

Jennings, M. *The Art and Science of Co-Teaching*. Las Vegas: National Conference on Differentiation, 2011.

Jensen, E. *Brain-Compatible Strategies*. Del Mar, CA: Turning Point, 1997.

Jensen, E. *Different Brains, Different Learners*. Thousand Oaks, CA: Corwin Press, 2000.

Jensen, E. *Teaching with the Brain in Mind,* 2nd ed. Alexandria, VA: ASCD, 2005.

Johnson, D., and Johnson, R. *Joining Together: Group Theory and Group Skills,* 5th ed. Boston: Allyn & Bacon, 1994.

Kagan, S. *Kagan Cooperative Learning*. San Clemente, CA: Kagan Cooperative Learning, 1994.

Karge, B. D., McClure, M., and Patton, P. L. "The Success of Collaboration: Resource Programs for Students with Disabilities in Grades 6 Through 8." *Remedial and Special Education* 16, no. 2 (1995): 79–89.

Kartan, T. *Inclusion Strategies That Work! Research-Based Methods for the Classroom*. Thousand Oaks, CA: Corwin Press, 2005.

Kaugeldt, M. *Begin with the Brain: Orchestrating the Learner-Centered Classroom*. Tuscon, AZ: Sephyr Press, 1999.

Knackendoffel, E. A. "Collaborative Teaming in the Secondary School." In *Teaching Adolescents with Learning Disabilities: Strategies and Methods,* 2nd ed., edited by D. D. Deshler, E. S. Ellis, and B. K Lenz, 579–615. Denver: Love Publishing, 1996.

Knackendoffel, E. "Collaborative Teaming in the Secondary School." *Focus on Exceptional Children* 40, no. 4 (2007): 1.

Kronberg, R. "Co-Teaching Institute." Joliet, IL: Joliet Public School District, 2008.

Kryza, K. *Practical Inclusion Strategies: Maximizing Student Success in the Inclusive Classroom (Grades 6–12)* Bellevue, WA: Bureau of Education and Research, 2007.

Least Restrictive Environment Coalition. *Still Waiting, After All These Years... Inclusion of Children with Special Needs in New York City Public Schools.* New York: Least Restrictive Environment Coalition, 2001.

Marzano, R. J. *Building Background Knowledge for Academic Achievement.* Alexandria, VA: ASCD, 2004.

Marzano, R., Pickering, D., and Pollock, J. *Classroom Instruction That Works: Research-Based Strategies for Increasing Student Achievement.* Alexandria, VA: ASCD, 2001.

Murawski, W., and Dieker, L. "Tips and Strategies for Co-Teaching at the Secondary Level." *Teaching Exceptional Children* 36, no. 5 (2004): 52–8.

Murawski, W.W. *Co-Teaching in the Inclusive Classroom: Working Together to Help All Your Students Find Success (Grades 6–12).* Bellevue, WA: Bureau of Education and Research, 2004.

Murawski, W. W. *Collaborative Teaching in Secondary Schools: Making the Co-Teaching Marriage Work!* Thousand Oaks, CA: Corwin Press, 2009.

Murawski, W. W. *Collaborative Teaching in Elementary Schools: Making the Co-Teaching Marriage Work!* Thousand Oaks, CA: Corwin Press, 2010.

Nordlund, M. *How to Intensify Individualized Instruction for All Students (Grades K–8).* Midwest Conference on Differentiation. Chicago: Staff Development for Educators, 2011.

Ogle, D. M. "K-W-L: A Teaching Model That Develops Active Reading of Expository Text." *Reading Teacher* 39 (1986): 564–70.

Opitz, M. F. *Flexible Grouping in Reading: Practical Ways to Help All Students Become Better Readers.* New York: Scholastic, 1998.

Perez, K. *More Than 100 Brain-Friendly Tools and Strategies for Literacy Instruction.* Thousand Oaks, CA: Corwin Press, 2008.

Raywid, M. A. "Finding Time for Collaboration." *Educational Leadership* 51, no. 1 (1993): 30–4.

Reavis, G. *The Animal School.* Peterborough, NH: Crystal Springs, 1999.

Smutny, J., Walker, S., and Meckstroth, E. *Teaching Young Gifted Children in the Regular Classroom.* Minneapolis, MN: Free Spirit, 1997.

Sonbuchner, G. *Help Yourself: How to Take Advantage of Your Learning Styles.* New York: New Readers Press, 1991.

The Power of Two: Making a Difference Through Co-Teaching (video). Port Chester, NY: National Professional Resources, 1996.

Tomlinson, C. *The Differentiated Classroom: Responding to the Needs of All Learners.* Alexandria, VA: ASCD, 1999. ED 429 944

Tomlinson, C. A. *How to Differentiate Instruction in Mixed-Ability Classrooms.* Alexandria, VA: ASCD, 2001.

Van Denburg, A. *On the Fly Toolbox.* Fairfax, VA: Fairfax County Public Schools, Department of Special Services, 2000.

Vaughn, J., and Estes, T. *Reading and Reasoning Beyond the Primary Grades*. Needham Heights, MA: Allyn & Bacon, 1986.

Walther-Thomas, C., Bryant, M., and Land, S. "Planning for Effective Co-Teaching: The Key to Successful Inclusion." *Remedial and Special Education* 17 (1996): 255–65.

Wiggins, G., and McTighe, J. *Understanding by Design*. 2nd ed. Alexandria, VA: ASCD, 2005.

Winebrenner, S. *Teaching Kids with Learning Difficulties in the Regular Classroom: Strategies and Techniques Every Teacher Can Use to Challenge and Motivate Struggling Students*. Minneapolis, MN: Free Spirit, 1996.

Wood, J. *Adapting Instruction for Mainstreamed and at-Risk Students*. Columbus, OH: Merrill, 1992.

York-Barr, J., Kronberg, R., and Doyle, M. B. *A Shared Agenda for General and Special Educators Participant Guide*. Baltimore: Paul H. Brookes, 1996.

Web Resources

www.lrecoalition.org (Least Restrictive Environment Coalition)

www.powerof2.org

www.randomactsofkindness.org

www.teachtolerance.org

www.operationrespect.org

http://nichcy.org (National Dissemination Center for Children with Disabilities)

www.aimhieducational.com/inclusion

www.ldonline.org

www.writedesignonline.com

www.teach-nology.com

www.cec.eped.org

Index

Book reports, 199
Brainstorming: for problem solving, 99

C

Centers. *See* Station teaching
Central auditory processing disorder (CAPD), 11
Chart Chatter activity, 222
Choice boards, 189, 196
Choices, for students: activities to promote, 196–197; grouping and, 108; guidelines for, 119; importance of, 196
Choral reading, 189
Chunked curriculum, 121
CI. *See* Cognitively impaired students
Class combinations, 70
Class sizes, 43
Classroom environment: administrators' support for, 144; assessment of, 90; co-teaching checklist regarding, 38–39; meeting students' needs in, 121; modification/accommodation checklist for, 158; physical organization of, 107; small-group learning in, 109; for station teaching, 214; students' perspective of, 121; supporting special needs students in, 165–169; tips for, 84
Classroom management: collaborative planning for, 120; co-teaching checklist regarding, 38; co-teaching implementation planning and, 41–42; roles and responsibilities for, 52, 53, 55; teachers' assessment of, 92
Classroom meetings, 105
Classroom rules, 123
Cliques, 70
Coaching: observation as, 17
Cognitively impaired (CI) students, 11
Collaboration: assessment of, 66; challenges related to, 95; for classroom management, 120; classroom rules for, 123; conflict management to maintain, 97–98; in co-teaching implementation, 45; in framework for co-teaching, 5; importance of, 65; tips for fostering, 65. *See also* Planning time
Communication: about small-group activities, 112; classroom board for, 84; co-teaching checklist regarding, 40; in co-teaching implementation, 36, 45; to evaluate co-teaching process, 100–102; feedback cards for, 157; importance of, 100; to manage conflict, 97–98; overcoming issues involving,

61–66; during planning time, 84; for problem solving, 99; roles and responsibilities for, 53; self-assessment of, 90
Communication cards, 101–102
Communication disorders, 168
Communication specialists, 141
Community of learners: enhancing inclusion in, 104–105; establishing behavioral norms in, 123; factors involved in creating, 104; online resources related to, 106
Compliance issues, 94
Comprehension, 223–230
Comprehension-level questions, 204, 208
Concept skits, 227
Conflict management, 97–99
Consistency, 124
Consultants, co-teaching, 35
Content modifications, 159–160
Continuum of services: definition of, 11; scheduling guidelines and, 138
Conversation starters, 62–63
Cooperative learning, 9
Co-teaching: anticipation guide for, 13; approaches to, 16; assumptions about, 13; barriers to, 133; beginning stages of, 14; benefits of, xvi, 6–9; challenges of, 43–44; characteristics of, 3, 82; definition of, 3–4, 11; evaluation of, 100–102; forming teams for, 83; framework for, 5; implementation process for, 35–50; location of, 10; maintaining effective, 232; misconceptions about, 4; preimplementation considerations, 10; preparation checklist for, 38–40; roles and responsibilities in, 51–56; stages of, 233–236; teachers' lack of knowledge about, 1; terminology related to, 11–12
Co-teaching models: application of, 31–33; for large-group instruction, 17–20; listing of, 16; selection of, 36–37; for small-group instruction, 21–26; variations of, 27–30
Co-Teaching Observation Form, 144, 146
Counselors, 142
Creativity: benefits of co-teaching for, 6; planning tips, 45
Cubing, 200–208
Cubing Companion Activity Sheet, 207
Culminating reviews, 230
Cultural differences: sharing of, 105; small-group activities and, 112

Culture, of school: assessment of, 132; barriers to co-teaching and, 133; in framework for co-teaching, 5

Curriculum: adaptations to, 162; chunking of, 121; planning tips, 45; teachers' competence in, 91

D

Data collection, 17

Decision making, 93; adaptation flow chart for, 154; administrators' support for, 143

Differential standards, 149

Differentiated products, 195, 200

Difficulty, modifications to, 149, 161

Direct instruction, 59, 158

Directions, giving, 59, 160, 176

Discipline: co-teaching checklist regarding, 39; establishing norms for, 123

Discussions, 221, 247

Distracted students, 174

Double-entry journals, 213

Duet teaching: description of, 28; example of, 31

Dyscalculia, 12

Dysgraphia, 12

Dyslexia: definition of, 12; online resources for, 106

Dyspraxia, 12

E

Early dismissal days, 73

EBD. *See* Emotional-behavioral disorder

Educational diagnostician, 141

Elementary schedules, 68

E-mail, 48

Emergency tasks cards, 189

Emotional situations, 64

Emotional-behavioral disorder (EBD), 11

Empowering students, 105

Engagement, of students: benefits of co-teaching for, 9; tips for increasing, 189–190

English, 201

Enhancements, 149–150

Enrichment activities, 117

Evaluation-level questions, 205, 208

Every-Pupil Response Techniques, 224

Exit cards, 227–228

Expectations, of students: benefits of co-teaching for, 8; classroom rules and, 124; for independent work, 116

Expert helpers, 110

F

Faculty meetings, 48; for expanding planning times, 73

Fairness, xvii

Family Feud game, 230

FBA. *See* Functional behavior assessment

Feedback, for co-teachers, 64; from administrators, 145; communication cards for, 157

Feedback, for students: in small-group activities, 110; in Speak and Add model, 27

Finishing work, 172

Finland, education in, xv

First Days of School (Wong & Wong), xv

504 plan, 11

Flexibility, of teachers, 96

Focus students, 17

Four-Square Quick-Write activity, 228

Friend, M., 16

Frustration, 97

Functional behavior assessment (FBA), 12

Furniture, classroom, 107

G

General education teachers: in Adapting Curriculum model, 29; in alternative teaching, 25–26; benefits of co-teaching for, 6, 7; challenges of, 94; in co-teaching models, 18, 19; introduction of, 57; roles and responsibilities of, 51–56, 58–60; sample duties of, 55. *See also* Teachers, co-teaching

Goal setting: adaptations to, 161; assessment of, 91; benefits of co-teaching for, 9; by co-teachers, 134; schedule creation and, 138; tool for, 118

Grade-level teams, 143

Grades: co-teaching checklist regarding, 40; guidelines for, 186; IEP and, 186; for modified assessments, 185

Graphic organizers: definition of, 209; online resources for, 106; rationale for, 210; to summarize learning, 228; tips for use of, 211; types of, 209, 212–213

Grouping students: for alternative teaching, 25; co-teaching checklist regarding, 38; co-teaching implementation process and, 36; co-teaching location and, 10; flexibility in, 108; modifications/accommodations for, 160; for parallel teaching, 23; planning for, 76; for skill group teaching, 27; for station teaching, 21

Guided practice, 117

H

Handouts, 59

Hands-on activities: benefits of co-teaching for, 6; in parallel teaching, 23

Headline Summary activity, 190

Help Wanted sheet, 117

Herringbone graphic organizers, 212

Highlight Vocabulary activity, 224

History simulations, 228–229

Hollywood Squares game, 230

Homework collection, 58

I

IDEA. *See* Individuals with Disabilities Education Act

Idea Wave activity, 227

Incentives, for teachers, 73

Inclusion: challenges of, xvi; versus co-teaching, 4; definition of, 4, 12; online resources related to, 106; requirements of, 1; tips for enhancing community and, 104–105

Incomplete work, 172

Independent activities, 60; expectations of students during, 116; learning materials for, 116; procedures for, 116; student support during, 117; tips for success in, 117

Individualized Education Plan (IEP): challenges related to, 94; co-teaching checklist regarding, 39; definition of, 12; grades and, 186; modifications versus differential standards and, 149; roles and responsibilities for, 52, 53, 54, 55, 56

Individuals with Disabilities Education Act (IDEA): continuum of services and, 11; definition of, 12; inclusion and, 12; least restrictive environment and, 12

Input, modifying, 155, 161

INSERT Coding Strategy, 224–225

Instruction: benefits of co-teaching for, 6–9; in framework for co-teaching, 5; teachers' assessment of, 91–92; teachers' role in, 58

Instructional delivery, 149

Instructional routines, 46

Interests, of students, 108, 127–130

Interim reports, 53

Interpersonal activities, 192

Interventions: definition of, 148; selection of, 188; tips for successful, 247. *See also specific interventions*

Intrapersonal activities, 193

Isolation, of teachers, xvi

I-statements, 64, 97

J

Jeopardy review, 189, 230

Journals, 213

K

Keyboard Curriculum activity, 190

Kinesthetic learners, 177, 193

Knowledge-level questions, 204, 208

L

Language arts activities, 223–230. *See also specific activities*

Language impairment, 170

Large-group instruction: models for, 17–20; planning tool for, 115; tips for facilitating, 114

Last Word activity, 229

Lead teachers: in co-teaching models, 17–19; misconceptions of co-teaching and, 4

Learned helplessness, 9

Learning centers. *See* Station teaching

Learning contracts, 189, 218

Learning disability, students with: definition of, 12; online resources for, 106; placement of, 136, 137; referrals to student study teams for, 138–139; small-group activities for, 112; strategies for supporting, 166–167, 170, 171

Learning line-ups, 192

Learning materials: for assessment modifications, 184; for independent work, 116; for modification toolkit, 156; modification/accommodation checklist for, 159; online resources for, 106; physical environment and, 107; planning for, 76; procedures for, 116; roles and responsibilities for, 52; in station teaching, 21; for supporting students with special needs, 165–169

Learning profiles, 181–182

Learning strategies: benefits of co-teaching for, 7, 8, 9; in co-teaching models, 19; planning for, 76; roles and responsibilities related to, 55

Password game, 230
Patience, 105
Peer tutoring, 9
Perez, K., xv, xvi
Personalities, of co-teachers, 87–89, 94
Physical impairments, 167–168
Picture It! activity, 190
Picture Personification activity, 229
Planning time: for Adapting Curriculum model, 29; administrators' support for, 144; agenda for, 76, 246; challenges related to, 95; components of, 74; co-teachers' sharing of, 84; co-teaching checklist regarding, 38; for duet teaching, 28; effective use of, 74; finding enough, 48, 73; for implementation of co-teaching, 41–42, 45–53; issues to discuss during, 120; minimum amount needed for, 45; ongoing tasks for, 47; roles and responsibilities for, 52; schedule for, 71, 74, 84; for small-group activities, 112; teachers' assessment of, 91; tips and tricks for, 45, 84, 245; for unit lessons, 49; weekly guide for, 47; worksheet for, 75. *See also* Collaboration
Positive attitude, 64, 98
Positive behaviors, 124
Positive language, 105
Posters, 190
Predict a Passage activity, 222
Prereading activities, 221–222
Preteaching, 60, 65
Previewing strategies, 222
Principals, 140
Problem-solving steps, 99
Procedures, classroom: benefits of, 77, 119; classroom environment and, 107; guidelines for setting up, 119; importance of, 77; for independent work, 116; for learning materials, 116; to seek support, 117; strategies for success in, 122; types of, 77–78
Process-oriented lessons, 18
Professional development: administrators' support for, 143; co-teaching preimplementation considerations related to, 10, 35; critical components of, 134
Professional satisfaction, 6, 7
Proximity techniques, 65, 124, 174
Psychologists, 141

Q

Quantity, adaptation of, 149, 161
Question and Quick Write activity, 189

Question Card Relay activity, 229
Question prompts, 204–205, 208
Quick Write activity, 189
Quote Card Match activity, 222

R

Readiness, of students, 108
Reading lessons: modification/accommodation checklist for, 159; in parallel teaching, 23. *See also specific activities*
Reading strategies, 221–230
Reavis, G., xvii
Recess, 73
Reflection: activities to support students', 227, 228; to guide intervention selection, 188; on modifications, 155; during planning time, 76
Reframing actions/thoughts, 97
Reinforcing positive behaviors, 124, 189
Remedial programs: alternative teaching as, 25; negative effects of, xvi, 10; roles and responsibilities for, 53; shortcomings of, 1
Resource managers, 174
Respect, 123
Response cards, 174, 224
Response to intervention (RTI), 12
Reteaching, 60
Review games, 230
Rhyme, Rhythm, Rap activity, 190
Rhythmic activities, 190, 191–192
Risk taking, 105
Roaming teachers, 18, 19
Role models, 36
Routines, classroom: benefits of, 77, 119; classroom environment and, 107; co-teaching checklist regarding, 39; guidelines for setting up, 119, 120; importance of, 77; planning time and, 46; to support students with special needs, 166, 167
RTI. *See* Response to intervention
Rubrics, 106
Rules, classroom, 123–124

S

Scaffolding: definition of, 12; planning for, 76
Scanning, 159
Schedules: administrators' support for, 143; challenges related to, 79; complexity of, 68; co-teaching preimplementation considerations related to, 10, 35; for elementary students, 68; general considerations related to, 68; guiding

pointers related to, 43; co-teaching preimplementation considerations related to, 10; flexibility of, 96; incentives for, 73; maintaining effective partnership between, 232; overcoming communication issues between, 61–66; partner selection of, 36; personalities of, 87–89; planning of future program by, 242; relationship building between, 85; role of, on student study teams, 140; self-assessment of, 86, 235–241; sharing of students by, 96. *See also* General education teachers; Special education teachers

Teacher-student ratios, 23

Teaching responsibilities: co-teaching checklist regarding, 38; co-teaching implementation and, 41; co-teaching pointers related to, 43

Teaching styles: alternative teaching and, 25; assessment of, 90–92; challenges related to, 94

Team decision making, 93

Team posters, 190

Team teaching: versus co-teaching, 4; model for, 20

Teams, co-teaching: assessment of, 87–92; characteristics of, 82; definition of, 81; formation of, 83; personalities of, 87–89; relationship building for, 85; self-assessment of, 86; shared planning time for, 84

Teamwork: definition of, 81; negotiation for, 84; during planning time, 84

Test administration, 59

Textbooks, 159

Text-Talk Summary activity, 190

Think-Tac-Toe activity, 189, 196–197

Time restraints, 95, 149, 161, 172

Tone, of voice, 98

Tool kits, 29

Tourette syndrome, 12

Transitions, 78; for small-group activities, 111; tips for smooth, 122

Trust: America's educational system and, xv; for effective teamwork, 85; Finland's educational system and, xv

U

Underexplaining, 189

Understanding, checking for, 223

Unit lessons: online resources for, 106; planning form for, 49; planning tips for, 45, 46; scheduling considerations and, 69

V

Values, of teachers, 63, 94

Verb list, 208

Verbal activities, 193–194

Visual activities, 191

Visual aids: for communication, 84; for procedures, 77–78; in Speak and Add model, 27

Visual impairments, 168

Visual instruction plans (VIPs), 221, 224

Visual learners, 177, 191

Vocabulary activities, 198, 224

Volunteers, 48

Voting, 189

W

Walls of wonder, 105

Warm-ups, 65

Washington State Department of Education, 106

Weekly planning guides, 47

Whip Around activity, 189

Who Wants to Be a Millionaire? game, 230

Whole-group instruction, 6

Wong, H., xv–xvi

Wong, R., xv

Word Sort activity, 222

Word Theater activity, 229

Word Window activity, 224

Work assignments, 107, 172, 195

Writer's workshop, 46

Writing assignments, 174–175

Written tests, 173, 184

Y

Y-chart activity, 110